Walking in Snowdonia
Volume 1

On the Priest's Path above Nant Ffrancon

Walking in
Snowdonia

Volume 1

Carl Rogers

MARA BOOKS

First published in April 2000 by **Mara Books**,
22 Crosland Terrace, Helsby, Cheshire WA6 9LY.
Telephone: 01928 723744

This new fully revised edition published by
Mara Books, May 2005

All enquiries regarding sales telephone: 01928 723744

ISBN 1-902512-06-5

Acknowledgements
Special thanks to Bob Nash for checking all the route descriptions and Snowdonia National Park for advice on the use of specific footpaths and general rights of way.

British Library Cataloguing-in-publication data. A catalogue is available for this book from the British Library.

Whilst every effort has been made to ensure that the information in this book is correct, the author or the publisher can accept no responsibility for errors, loss or injury however caused.

Maps based on out of copyright Ordnance Survey mapping.

Contents

Location of the walks

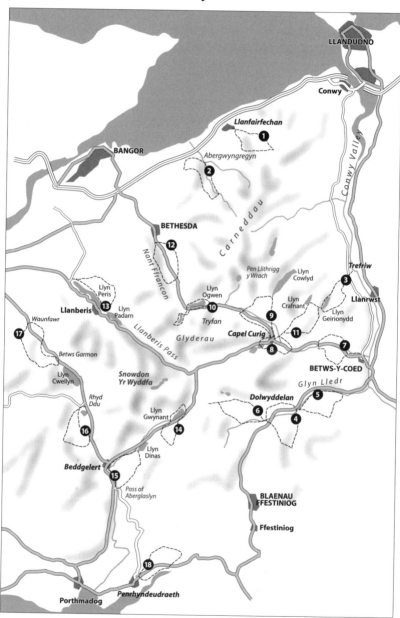

Introduction

S NOWDONIA is one of Britain's most rugged and beautiful mountain areas—fourteen peaks exceed 3,000 feet, whilst Snowdon itself (Yr Wyddfa) can lay claim to being the highest and grandest mountain in Britain south of the Scottish Highlands. In ancient times these mountains were known as Eryri—'the highlands' and presented early settlers and travellers with a harsh inhospitable mountain barrier. The more familiar English name—Snowdon—is thought to have come from the Saxon word 'Snaudune' meaning 'snowy hills' and was allegedly bestowed by Dark Age Saxon invaders who viewed the mountains from the lowlands to the east and believed them to be perpetually snow covered.

Snowdon and Moel Siabod from the eastern side of the Conwy Valley

The fickle nature of our climate, along with the close proximity of the Gulf Stream, ensure that these mountains are rarely snow covered for long periods today. At times however, severe winter weather transforms them into Alpine-like summits of great beauty. In fact it was glaciers like those to be found in the Alps, that are responsible for the appearance of Snowdonia today. At its greatest extent, ice up to 3,000 feet thick is thought to have formed a great dome or ice cap to the east of the central mountain area and under this weight numerous glacier tongues were forced outwards between the high summits carving the rocky, steep-sided mountain valleys which we see today. The Llanberis Pass, Conwy Valley, Glyn Lledr, Nant Ffrancon and Nant Gwynant are fine examples. It is these beautiful mountain valleys and the lower hillsides, rather than Snowdonia's rocky summits, which are the subject of this book.

Snowdonia National Park includes within its boundaries all the major peaks in Wales north of the Dyfi estuary, along with many of its most beautiful valleys. This volume deals with the northern half of Snowdonia bounded by the Conwy Valley to the east, Glyn Lledr and the Vale of Ffestiniog to the south, with Cwm Pennant forming the western limit. This is probably the best known and most popular part of Snowdonia and offers some of the most spectacular scenery. All the peaks which exceed 3,000 feet are to be found here, along with a number of large mountain lakes. Although few of these can rival the great fjord-like meres of the Lake District, we do have such delights as Llyn Crafnant, cradled in its hidden valley and surrounded by steep crags and peaceful woodlands; the pastoral beauty of Llyn Gwynant reflecting the shapely cone of Yr Aran and surrounding woods, and the mysterious Llyn Dinas, taking its name from the Dark Age fortress associated with Merlin and Vortigern which overlooks it. Llyn Padarn and Llyn Peris at the foot of the Llanberis Pass may carry the scars of two centuries of slate quarrying but they still provide attractive foregrounds for some of the finest and most famous views of the Snowdon group. The classic view of Snowdon, Y Lliwedd and Crib Goch from the

The Snowdon group from Llynnau Mymbyr

shore of Llynnau Mymbyr at Capel Curig is surely one of the most famous and most photographed mountain views in Britain.

Another feature of the fine walking to be enjoyed in the valleys and lower hillsides of Snowdonia is the superb views of the adjacent peaks. After decades spent wandering Snowdonia's highest skylines I have found these unusual and sometimes superior views to be the highlight of most of the walks. The best view of any mountain is rarely from the valley, or even from the summit of a neighbouring peak, but often from across the valley at about half height—like viewing the Matterhorn from the Gornergrat, or Mount Blanc from the Aiguille Rouge. The views of Tryfan from walk 9, Moel Siabod and the Snowdon group from the path to Llyn Crafnant on walk 11 and Snowdon, Y Lliwedd and Yr Aran from the pass on walk 6 are fine examples.

A brief history

THE mountains, hills and valleys of Snowdonia, like much of Britain before the Roman conquest, were originally clothed in thick woodlands; mainly sessile oak which can still be seen on uncultivated hillsides here and there today. This tree cover only thinned out towards the higher summits, on the steeper craggy slopes and on exposed coastal headlands where the salt wind prevented growth. This resulted in a forested landscape which is a far cry from the often barren, treeless expanses which have come to epitomise the highland areas of not just Wales, but Britain as a whole. The woods which do exist in highland areas today are more likely to be non-indigenous conifer plantations contained by straight fence lines which traverse the landscape for miles ignoring the natural contours of the land.

When the first settlers came to Britain, the coastal areas were the only practical locations for habitation; as a result, the earliest man made signs of settlement—neolithic structures—occur almost exclusively along the coastal plains and lower valleys. Nearby Anglesey and Lleyn are covered in such remains but very few are found in the inland area which we now call Snowdonia, for the simple reason that it was, for the most part, impenetrable. By the Bronze Age, however, things were different. The introduction of grazing animals and a change in the climate prevented the regrowth of cleared woodland at higher levels. A number of Bronze Age cairns exist on the summits of the highest peaks in the area, notably those on the Carneddau, although these are not thought to indicate the existence of dwellings at this altitude. However, the presence of so many burial mounds, along with the considerable man power required to work the copper mines at the Great Orme, do indicate a large population in and around the Conwy Valley during the Bronze Age. Items made here and at the earlier stone axe factory at Penmaenmawr have been found all over the British Isles, indicating a fairly developed system of trading.

There is little indication that these Bronze Age inhabitants had any need for defensive settlements or forts, which is why we know so little about where they lived. They seem to have lived a semi nomadic life of cattle and sheep rearing requiring little in the way of permanent habitation.

The next phase of settlement is known as the Iron Age and is very different in that one of the most common legacies from this period is the hill fort. They most often occur on lower hilltops close to the coast, but there are many examples further inland—notably above the Conwy Valley and along the Glaslyn above Beddgelert and Llyn Dinas—indicating colonisation of the highland valleys in the centuries before the Roman Conquest. In addition to hill forts, hut circles are also associated with this period. These consist of the stone foundations of huts which had wigwam-type roofs and sides. They occur both singly and in groups, either on their own or within hill forts. They suit both settled and seasonal migration settlement styles and are found today all over the area.

By the time of the Roman conquest, the hills, mountains and valleys of Snowdonia could well have had a sizeable population but it was not the conquest of these rebellious hill tribes which first brought the Roman armies here—it was the Druids on nearby Anglesey. Little is really know about the Druids. What is almost certain however, is that they were the main instigators in stirring up resistance to Roman rule and it was this that resulted in their destruction. Their beliefs and religious rituals are the subject of much imagination and debate, but they wrote none of their teachings down, committing all to memory and oral teaching. As a result everything died with them.

By AD 45 the Romans had a fort at Chester on what is now the Welsh border, but it took another sixteen years for them to penetrate the highland area of North Wales. This came in AD 61 when general Suetonius Paulinus, with an army of 10,000, marched west along what was even then a recognised route into the mountains. This route entered our area near Tal-y-Cafn in the Conwy Valley before rising to a high pass between the villages of Llanfairfechan and Rowen known as Bwlch-y-Ddeufaen ('pass of the two stones'). It then descended to Aber and continued along the coastal plain giving access to Anglesey across the Menai Strait. When the soldiers arrived at the Menai Strait the Druids were waiting on the far shore with hoards of naked, painted warriors and women shouting defiance at the invaders. The historian Tacitus gives the following account of the scene:

One of the Bronze Age standing stones at Bwlch-y-Ddeufaen

'By the far shore stood an opposing battle-line, thick with men and weapons, women running between them like the Furies in their funeral clothes, their hair flowing, carrying torches; and Druids among them pouring out frightful curses with their hands raised high to the heavens, our soldiers being so scared by the unfamiliar sight that their limbs were paralysed, and they stood motionless and exposed to be wounded.'

The soldiers, unnerved at first, were urged on by their general and eventually crossed the Strait to an easily won victory. The Druid priesthood were massacred on the spot and their sacred groves burned to the ground. Triumph was short lived however, Suetonious and his armies had to return quickly to the south of Britain to deal with the rebellion of Queen Boudicea. It was Agricola who, in AD 77, more fully subdued Anglesey and established a permanent presence in the area.

The Romans established two main centres in North Wales, forts at Caernarfon and Tomen-y-Muir to the south near Trawsfynydd. In addition, smaller camps positioned along routes between these forts have been found at Pen y Gwryd, near the head of the Llanberis Pass; on the south bank of Afon Llugwy between Betws-y-Coed and Capel Curig; and in the Conwy Valley at Caerhun close to the ford at Tal-y-Cafn. This shows that there were routes through the mountains in regular use throughout the Roman period.

In the late fourth century the Roman armies left Britain and the country entered a period of decay and political disarray. Most of the stories from Wales during this early period are difficult to separate from the myths which surround such characters as King Arthur and Merlin.

One of the most important sites from this time is a small craggy hill close to Beddgelert known as Dinas Emrys. Little is known about the site for sure but one of the most important and colourful stories from the Dark Ages is associated with it. Following the withdrawal of the Romans from Britain, the island was left unguarded and it was soon being attacked and plundered by

Dinas Emrys

Picts in the north from beyond Hadrian's Wall and Irish from the west. The king of Britain at that time was Vortigern (now thought to be more of a title such as 'Caesar' than a personal name) and in an attempt to ward off these attacks, he enlisted the help of mercenaries from the among the Germanic tribes on the Continent. This was successful at first, but the influx of these tribes could not be halted and they soon began to set up their own kingdoms. All attempts to expel them failed. Vortigern was blamed and fled west to the remote highland of Eryri where he tried to establish a fortress at Dinas Emrys.

The story up to this point seems to be based mainly on historic events but myth now takes over. All Vortigern's attempts to build a fortress at Dinas Emrys fail. Each time the walls are constructed they either fall or crumble and none of the builders know why. Vortigern consults his councillors and wise men who inform him that the only way to make the building work a success is to sacrifice a boy with no father on the site and mix his blood with the mortar (perhaps an echo of earlier Druid practices). Messengers are sent out, a fatherless boy is found in South Wales and brought to Vortigern.

The boy shows great wisdom when speaking to Vortigern's councillors and offers an alternative reason for the failure of Vortigern's building plans. He tells them that if they look beneath the paving on the hill they will find two serpents, one white, the other red. Once released they would fight, the white serpent almost defeating the red, before the red serpent finally puts the white serpent to flight. The two serpents and the pool are discovered beneath the paving as predicted and when released they begin to fight. The red serpent, after almost suffering defeat, finally triumphed as the boy had said.

The young boy then explains the meaning of these events. The two serpents represent two nations and the pool Vortigern's kingdom. The white serpent stands for the Saxon invaders who were close, at that time, to overthrowing the red serpent of the British. The final victory of the red serpent represents the final victory of the British over the Saxons who would then be forced to return from where they came. He then gave his name: Ambrosius. The hill and the fortress to be built there would become his and Vortigern was to leave. Curiously Vortigern seems to have taken this advise and no more is heard of him. Some stories say that he retired to a remote valley on the Lleyn Peninsula which still bears his name—Nant Gwrtheyrn, meaning 'Vortigern's Valley'.

Investigation of Dinas Emrys has revealed a long history of occupation reaching back to the pre-Roman period. The only visible remains today are those of a twelfth century tower, but other finds indicate that there were indeed occupants and thus possibly a fortress contemporary with Vortigern. Interestingly, the name Dinas Emrys, translated means the 'fortress' or 'city of Emrys' (Emrys is the Welsh version of the Romanised name Ambrosius).

The other site of Dark Age importance is in the north of the area overlooking the mouth of Afon Conwy. Here, a fortress existed for over 700 years before Edward I built his more famous castle across the river at Conwy. Far more is known about this site than Dinas Emrys.

While the east coast of Britain was being colonised by Angles, Saxons and Jutes the west was under attack from the Irish. In an attempt to prevent the Irish from colonising what is now Wales, a Celtic Chieftain called Cunedda Wledig and his warrior sons came from Strathclyde in the north of Britain bringing with them a large fighting force. Cunedda settled at Aberffraw on Anglesey and established the kingdom of Gwynedd, along with a dynasty which would rule Gwynedd until the conquest of Edward I. The Irish were finally defeated and expelled from Wales by Cunedda's grandson, Cadwallon Lawhir, in a final battle on Anglesey in AD 470.

It is not known for sure who built the first fortress at Deganwy, but by the time of Cadwallon's son, King Maelgwyn Gwynedd (510-547), a fortress of some note must have existed on the hilltop known today as The Vardre. Despite the fact that he is said to have been a wicked ruler, responsible for the murder of numerous relatives and rivals, it was during his reign that Christianity became firmly established in Gwynedd with the founding of monasteries at Penmon and Ynys Cybi (Holy Island) on Anglesey. By Maelgwyn's time, the Irish threat was but a faint memory and he was able to use a period of peace and stability to indulge in a hedonistic lifestyle rare for the time and which brought strong condemnation from the church. He is also remembered for his death from a yellow plague, which was seen by many as punishment for his wickedness and is said to have been foretold by the bard Taliesin, a contemporary of Maelgwyn.

The following centuries were far from peaceful and Gwynedd's rulers had to fight constantly to retain their kingdom. The Saxon colonisation of the south and east of Britain was swift and by the turn of the seventh century, Northumbrian Saxons had pushed as far west as the River Dee, where in AD 616 they won a decisive battle near Chester. This effectively severed the British—who would henceforth be known as the 'Welsh'—from their kinsmen in northern England and Cornwall and confine them to the land which we know today as Wales. The Saxons were unable to continue their conquest further west and in the following century, the Saxon king, Offa, built his famous dyke to mark the limit of Saxon control.

The Viking raids of the tenth century were particularly problematic for Wales but they resulted in few settlements. These restless pirates seem to have been more interested in plunder than in conquering the lands which they raided, but this was not true of the Normans who came onto the scene in 1066, the most well known date in our history books. Although their victory was won in a distant corner of Britain, their presence was soon felt in Wales and these new conquerors were not as

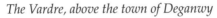

The Vardre, above the town of Deganwy

content as the Saxons had been to merely contain the Welsh beyond Offa's Dyke. Powerful and ambitious Marcher Lords were established along the border and encouraged to extend their control into Wales by what ever means they had.

This brought a time of intense conflict in Wales—not just with the Normans but also between the Welsh themselves. A major problem was that the Welsh never stood as a united nation against invaders—their real enemies. The country was composed of numerous of petty kingdoms whose rulers spent most of their time, resources and energy fighting rivals from within their own family or those of adjacent kingdoms. Welsh princes frequently allied themselves with Normans and Saxons against their own countrymen when it seemed convenient.

It was during this time that the highland region of Snowdonia became a place of refuge for the people of Gwynedd, one of the most powerful and enduring of the Welsh kingdoms. The people of Gwynedd proved to be particularly difficult to conquer because their way living and fighting enabled them to move their families and livestock into the upper mountain valleys at short notice. Their fighting style was perfectly compatible with their environment; lightly armed, they could move quickly in difficult terrain, but they wisely avoided open combat in the field with better equipped English armies.

The lands to the east, though more fertile and desirable, were harder to defend and the Normans were able to advance to Afon Clwyd where they established an early castle at Rhuddlan. From there, the push west was inevitably along the coast, but Afon Conwy presented a major obstacle. The fortress at Deganwy, which had been in continuous use for some 600 years, now proved to be inadequate being positioned on the wrong side of the river, however, the mountainous heartland of Snowdonia provided defence enough and time and time again the Welsh retreated into the high valleys leaving Norman armies without the means to feed themselves or the ability to exercise their superior fighting power developed for the open battlefields of

England and France. Both King John and Henry III suffered humiliation in this way in their wars against Llywelyn ap Iowerth (Llywelyn Fawr or Llywelyn the Great). By this time Deganwy had fallen into enemy hands so frequently that Llywelyn ap Gruffydd (grandson of Llywelyn Fawr) finally destroyed it in 1263.

Llywelyn's castle at Dolbadarn near Llanberis

Llywelyn Fawr, who ruled Gwynedd from the closing years of the twelfth century until his death in 1240, is perhaps the most famous of all the Welsh princes and the highland area of Snowdonia would have been particularly well known to him. He was born at Dolwyddelan in the Lledr Valley around 1170 and spent his early years with his mother's family in South Wales before returning as a young man to claim the throne of Gwynedd. As ruler of Gwynedd he would have moved constantly through his kingdom living at a number of courts and castles in such locations as Aber, Beddgelert, Trefriw, Dolbenmaen, Criccieth, Dolbadarn and Aberffraw. Despite his marriage to Princess Joan, the daughter of King John of England, he had a number of famous conflicts with his powerful father-in-law.

Llywelyn died in 1240 at the Abbey of Aberconwy which he had founded and was buried there. Despite his conflicts with the English he was able to pass on to his son a substantial kingdom. The native Welsh castles to be seen at Dolbadarn, Criccieth, Ewloe, Castell y Bere and Dolwyddelan today, date from this period and were originally built by Llywelyn.

Llywelyn's son Dafydd did not rule long and Gwynedd passed to the sons of Llywelyn's eldest illegitimate son Gruffydd, who had been imprisoned at Criccieth and the Tower of London by both his father and his brother. He died in a fall whilst trying to escape from the Tower of London. Gruffydd's sons were soon competing for the kingdom, but Llywelyn ap Gruffydd emerged victorious and is said to have imprisoned his eldest brother Owain at Dolbadarn for over 20 years. Llywelyn's other brother, Dafydd, proved to be more troublesome and even went over to the side of the English for a while.

Llywelyn (often called 'Llywelyn the Last' to distinguish him from his equally famous grandfather) spent most of his rule in conflict with the English and in particular Edward I who became king of England in 1277. He proved to be one of the strongest and most ruthless kings ever to sit on the English throne and insisted that Llywelyn paid homage during his coronation. When Llywelyn became suspicious and refused to do this, the two were rarely at peace again. Their final conflict was triggered by Llywelyn's treacherous brother Dafydd, who was dissatisfied with the lands Edward had given him for his support against Llywelyn. Together they took a number of border castles and soon had much of the territory which Llywelyn had lost to Edward under their control. In the early stages of the conflict Llywelyn was caught alone and killed at Builth Wells (possibly he was betrayed and led into a trap). Dafydd then assumed control but was unpopular and was eventually handed over to Edward by his own men.

Dafydd received a particularly gruesome punishment for his treachery. He was dragged through the streets of Shrewsbury

Conwy Castle, one of Edward I's fortresses

before being hung and disembowelled while still alive. After beheading his body was then quartered and the pieces displayed in towns throughout the kingdom. His head was sent to the Tower to be placed next to that of his brother Llywelyn. This was a punishment devised by Edward and reserved for those he considered to be traitors.

Edward followed up his victory by building a ring of castles around Snowdonia to control what had proved to be the most problematic part of Wales. The remains of these fortresses can be seen today and have become an unmistakeable part of the landscape of North Wales. Some of these castles were to play a part in the revolt of Owain Glyndwr, notably Harlech, where he had his headquarters for a number of years, but they were never to see the kind of conflict for which they were designed and by the sixteenth century the use of the cannon rendered them useless—one of the reasons they were so ineffective during the Civil War and to which many now owe their ruinous condition.

The Edwardian Conquest was not the final chapter in the Welsh struggle for independence though; this came with the revolt of Owain Glyndwr at the turn of the fifteenth century. Glyndwr came from the Dee valley close to the English border and had enjoyed a successful military career in the service of Richard II, before Richard was usurped by Henry Bolingbroke in 1399. By this time Glyndwr was in late middle age and seems, along with most of his nation, to have been suspicious of the new king. He then suffered a humiliating legal defeat in a dispute over land with his English neighbour Lord Grey of Ruthin, who was a favourite of the new king.

This seemingly minor event triggered the rebellion. The Welsh were quick to support Glyndwr and proclaimed him 'Prince of Wales'. His first move was to embark on a series of raids which included the burning of St Asaph church and the Ruthin estates of his rival Lord Grey. His ability to disappear into the mountains of Snowdonia following these raids gave rise to the belief that he possessed magical powers. In reality he was merely employing the same tactics which had enabled the Welsh to survive so well for the previous 1,000 years. He eventually captured Harlech Castle and made it his headquarters for the next five years.

Glyndwr almost achieved his dream of an independent Wales before his fortunes changed. Harlech fell, his supporters left his side and by 1409, nine years after his quarrel with Lord Grey, it was all over. The date and place of his death is not known—he simply vanished into the mountains as he had done so often before—another reason for his almost mythical reputation.

During the sixteenth and seventeenth centuries Snowdonia remained isolated by a poor road system and its few inhabitants supported themselves by cattle rearing on the ample highland pasture. By this time the woods which had originally covered much of the area had been cleared and the mountains and upland valleys would have appeared much as they do today.

One activity which would have been common at the time was the driving of surplus cattle to markets on the English border and many of the old paths which now cross high mountain passes would have been frequented by drovers.

Towards the end of this period small scale mining and quarrying had begun, particularly in the woods of Gwydir above the Conwy Valley. This was encouraged by entrepreneurs like Sir John Wynn from Gwydir, near Llanrwst and was the beginning of an industry which was to have a major impact on Snowdonia and would change the landscape dramatically during the eighteenth and nineteenth centuries.

Though mining was to continue at Gwydir for the next two and a half centuries it would never rival North Wales' most famous export—slate. Welsh slates had been regularly shipped to Ireland since the reign of Queen Elizabeth I and had been used even earlier to roof Chester Castle, but by the turn of the eighteenth century, trade with the Continent strengthened the industry and made quarrying a more lucrative business. Small private quarries were being worked above Llyn Padarn and Llyn

Peris in the early 1700s and from these, larger partnerships emerged enabling a large scale approach to be developed.

The other area where quality slate is accessible is in the neighbouring valley near the mouth of Nant Ffrancon. This land was part of the Penrhyn Estate and in 1765 the heiress married John Pennant, a wealthy sugar merchant from the West Indies. He immediately began to sell leases for quarrying in the area above the present location of Bethesda. His son Richard Pennant inherited the estate in 1781 and set about buying back the leases his father had sold until he had full control of all the quarrying on his land. This was the beginning of the Penrhyn Quarry.

Contemporary with this was the formation of the Dinorwig Slate Quarry formed in 1787. By 1791 Dinorwig was exporting two and a half million slates per year through the port at

The massive slate quarries above Llyn Peris

Caernarfon forcing Lord Penrhyn to build himself a port near Bangor. Narrow gauge railways ran between both ports and their respective quarries by the early 1800s.

All this activity had a major impact on this previously remote area. New villages and towns were built and the population doubled and in some cases trebled. One such town is Bethesda, which grew around the chapel a group of Non-Conformist quarry workers built for themselves on the banks of Afon Ogwen close to the Penrhyn Quarry. Similar chapels built at this time can be identified by their Biblical names, such as Nebo, Carmel and Bethel.

Another result of this activity was the improvement of the road system. At the beginning of the eighteenth century the roads in North Wales were little better than they had been 1,000 years earlier. The inner mountain area contained a few rough horse tracks mainly used by cattle drovers and shepherds. However, the increasing use of Holyhead as the port for Ireland highlighted the need for a good road through North Wales. Travellers were forced to take a route along the north coast negotiating dangerous crossings of Afon Conwy, Penmaenmawr, the Lafan Sands and finally the Menai Strait. An alternative route came via Pentrefoelas, crossing Afon Conwy at Llanrwst to reach Conwy, but travellers were still faced with Penmaenmawr and the Lafan Sands.

There was no route between Betws-y-Coed and Capel Curig, or any road through the Ogwen Valley prior to 1790 when Richard Pennant of Penrhyn built a coach road from Penrhyn up the west side of Nant Ffrancon, along the shore of Llyn Ogwen and through to Capel Curig on the edge of his estate. He also built 'The Royal Hotel' which is now 'Plas y Brenin Outdoor Centre'. In 1803 the Capel Curig Turnpike Trust built a link road between Capel Curig and Pentrefoelas. Coaches had been using the road to Pentrefoelas from London via Shrewsbury en-route to Holyhead for a number of years, but from there they turned north to Llanrwst because no suitable route west through the mountains existed. The Capel Curig link eliminated the need to pass through Conwy and negotiate the dangerous crossings of Penmaenmawr and the Lafan Sands. Mail coaches and travellers to Ireland immediately began to use this route.

All that remains of Pennant's old road through Ogwen

The Alpine-like East Face of Tryfan

Although the new route was an immediate success, the road itself was poorly constructed in places with steep gradients requiring passengers to leave the coach and walk or even push on the steepest sections. As a result, when Thomas Telford was commissioned to improve the road to Ireland, he followed the same route, but eliminated these dangerous sections—notably the descent to Betws-y-Coed from Pentrefoelas and the section along the west side of Nant Ffrancon.

This improved road system not only benefited commercial and political travellers (which had been the main reason for travelling in the past), it also opened up Snowdonia to the tourist. The writings of early travellers such as Thomas Pennant (from the same Flintshire family as the Pennants of Penrhyn) had raised awareness of the area, but now the journey could be made with greater ease, speed, safety and comfort. The hotels and inns which appeared along the mail route at Betws-y-Coed and Capel Curig provided the standard of accommodation which the wealthy traveller expected. In addition, the limit on Continental travel imposed by the Napoleonic Wars created a greater interest in British travel. Groups of artists established themselves at Betws-y-Coed and Capel Curig, among them the noted painter John Cox.

The coming of the railways in the mid-nineteenth century made the area even more accessible and although the Irish mail now went via rail along the coast, there were enough tourists visiting inner Snowdonia to compensate for this loss.

Such was the interest in Snowdonia and particularly Snowdon itself, being the highest mountain in England, Wales and Ireland, that a narrow gauge railway was built to carry visitors to the summit. It opened in 1895 and performed the function which had earlier been carried out by ponies.

Snowdonia did not just appeal to those who came here to paint, write or enjoy the mountains from the comfort of the valley or a train window. The rocky crests and crags of Snowdon, Tryfan and the Glyderau can, in detail, be every bit as challenging as the Alps, particularly during a hard winter and it was not long before Victorian Alpinists came to Snowdonia in preparation for their more ambitious plans abroad. The best known centres for mountaineers in Snowdonia during this period were the hotels at Pen-y-Gwryd and Pen-y-Pass (now a Youth Hostel) close to the head of the Llanberis Pass. Around these centres gathered a group of mountaineers who pioneered the exploration of Snowdonia's rock faces and developed the sport of rock climbing.

One of the most prominent names from the early decades of the twentieth century was James Meriman Archer Thompson. He and a number of companions—among them George Mallory of Everest fame—pioneered many of the early climbs on such

The Devil's Kitchen, Cwm Idwal

faces as Y Lliwedd, the east face of Tryfan and the Devil's Kitchen above Llyn Idwal.

Rock climbing reached new levels between the wars with such leading lights as Colin Kirkus and James Menlove Edwards who explored new harder climbs on some of the most difficult rock in Snowdonia. By today's standards these climbs are not particularly severe, but their exploratory nature and use of primitive equipment make them undertakings of the highest standard. Rock climbing as a sport has continued to develop and is now popular the world over, however, it owes its origins to the pioneers who first explored the dark crags of the Lake District and Snowdonia.

In the post war period the mountains ceased to be the preserve of the wealthy professional (who had previously been the only group to have the funds and the time available to spend on leisure pursuits). The availability and use of the motor car, along with the close proximity of the highly populated areas of Merseyside and Manchester brought the mountains within the grasp of the working classes. The establishing of climbing clubs, along with the use of old farm buildings as huts for cheap accommodation brought many more to the mountains for both walking and climbing. A trend which has continued.

The increased pressure this brought to bear on Snowdonia, along with the realisation of the value to the nation of our wild and beautiful places, led to the establishment of National Parks in Britain and the Snowdonia National Park came into being in 1951. Since then, the popularity of Snowdonia has continued to increase and visitors have doubled in number many times over. The result is that tourism accounts for a large portion of Snowdonia's income and will no doubt continue to do so.

Glossary of Welsh names

Aber	*river mouth*
Afon	*river*
Allt	*hillside*
Bach/fach	*little*
Bwlch	*gap, pass*
Bychan	*little*
Cae	*field, enclosure*
Caer	*fort*
Canol	*centre*
Capel	*chapel*
Carn, Carnedd	*heap of stones*
Carreg	*crag or stone*
Castell	*castle*
Cefn	*ridge*
Clogwyn	*cliff*
Coed	*wood*
Cors/cors	*bog or swamp*
Craig	*crag*
Crib	*jagged ridge*
Croes	*cross*
Cwm	*coombe*
Ddu/Du	*black*
Dinas	*city, fortress*
Dol/Ddol	*meadow*
Dyffryn	*valley*
Dwr	*water*
Eryri	*highland*
Esgair	*ridge*
Fawr/mawr	*large*
Felin	*mill*
Ffordd	*road*
Ffynnon	*well or fountain*
Foel	*bare hill*
Ffridd	*mountain pasture*
Galt	*slope*
Glan	*river bank*
Glas	*blue-green*
Glyn	*deep valley*
Goch/coch	*red*
Gwern	*alder coppice*
Gwyn	*white*
Hafod	*summer dwelling*
Hendre	*winter dwelling*
Hen	*old*
Isaf	*lower*
Llan	*church*
Llyn	*lake*
Llwyd	*grey*
Llys	*hall or court*
Lon	*lane*
Maen	*stone*
Maes	*field or meadow*
Moel	*rounded hill*
Mynach	*monk*
Mynydd	*mountain*
Newydd	*new*
Ogof	*cave*
Pant	*hollow*
Pen	*head or point*
Pennant	*valley head*
Penrhyn	*promontory*
Pistyll	*waterfall*
Plas	*house*
Pont	*bridge*
Pwll	*pool*
Rhaeadr	*waterfall*
Rhos	*moorland*
Rhyd	*ford*
Sarn	*causeway*
Tan	*below, under*
Tref	*town*
Twll	*cavern*
Twr	*tower*
Ty	*house*
Tyddyn	*farmstead*
Uchaf	*upper*
Wern	*alder swamp*
Y, Yr	*the*

Llanfairfechan

Distance: *5¹/₂ miles.*

A walk up onto the rounded shoulders of the Carneddau mountains to an ancient highway used in the days when the coast was all but inaccessible. Some steep sections in both ascent and descent. Good paths throughout.

Start: Begin the walk at Nant-y-Coed car park in Llanfairfechan. This can be reached by turning south at the traffic lights in the centre of Llanfairfechan ('Village Road'). Pass the Post Office and just before the bridge bear left into 'Bryn Road'. Higher up this becomes 'Valley Road'. Continue ahead (ignoring the right turn over the river), to the little car park for Nant-y-Coed immediately before the lane turns sharp left.

Grid ref: 694 740 (Landranger 115, Outdoor Leisure sheet 17).

The walk

1. Cross the footbridge over the river and turn left up 'Valley Road'. Follow the road passing another small car park and a few yards further on, bear left off the lane onto a signed footpath. The path forks in about 100 yards—bear right here onto a farm track which rises to a large metal field gate. About 50 yards before you reach the gate, turn left onto a signed footpath which rises up the bank with a field to your right. Cross a second track (metal gate to the right) and go up the bank straight ahead following the right of way along the left-hand field edge and bear left in the far corner. At the top of the field cross a stile and walk through a second field to a kissing gate. This leads into a large grazing

field where the path is less distinct. Take a direct line through the field eventually picking up a more obvious track.

Follow the track to a kissing gate in a stone wall which leads onto the open hillside. The path is not clear but the right of way heads for the obvious pass directly ahead (Bwlch-y-Ddeufaen) and runs parallel to the stream away to the right.

At the pass bear right along a stone wall to a track, where there is a ladder stile and gate.

Bwlch-y-Ddeufaen is the highest point reached by the old Roman road which linked the forts of Deva (Chester) and Segontium (Caernarfon). The road crossed Afon Conwy by a ford near Tal-y-Cafn, before rising steeply through the site of Rowen to the pass here at Bwlch-y-Ddeufaen. From here it continued across the northern slopes of the Carneddau to Abergwyngregyn, then made its way along the coastal plain to Segontium.

Although the Romans were the first to formalise this route across the mountains, they were certainly not its originators. Anglesey was famous throughout Europe as a centre for the Druid religion during the Celtic period and this, along with rich mineral reserves at Parys Mountain, would have made it important to Iron Age and Bronze Age settlers and attracted merchants from all over Britain. As the centre of the Druid religion it would have seen a steady stream of travellers, possibly from as far away as Brittany. Evidence for the antiquity of this route can be seen in the many prehistoric monuments which have been discovered along its length and are scattered all across these remote mountain sides. These monuments originate in remote periods of prehistory and include burial chambers, standing stones and stone circles.

Two standing stones thought to date from the Bronze Age period can be seen on the descent into the Conwy Valley and it is from these stones that the pass gets name—Bwlch-y-Ddeufaen means 'pass' or 'gap of the two stones'. The largest of the two stands about 300 yards from the stile on the south side of the road and is about eight feet high.

The first Romans to pass this way were the troops of Suetonius Paulinus who, in AD 61, advanced on Anglesey with over 10,000 men and slaughtered the Druids on the shores of the Menai Strait. With the establishing of the Roman fort at Caernarfon the road became an important communication link with the fort at Chester (Deva) and would have been in constant use throughout the Roman period. When roads were improved for the use of coaches during the late eighteenth century and a suitable route to Ireland via Holyhead was required, this road was found to be too difficult and dangerous and a lower coastal route favoured.

2. Turn right and follow the track as it contours the hillside for about 1½ miles.

As you round the northern spur of Yr Orsedd there is a prominent path to the right along the ridge to Craig Fawr and a little further on, the Roman road drops quite steeply on its descent to Abergwyngregyn. Turn right here at a signpost along the broad flat ridge and where the path forks, keep straight ahead indicated by the North Wales Path (NWP) sign. About 300 yards further on the path forks again, this time bear left following the NWP sign again (ignore the path straight ahead to Craig Fawr). This path takes you down below Craig Fawr skirting the upper edge of wall enclosed fields on the left.

Where the wall on your left bends left and the path forks again, keep straight ahead with a bird's eye view of Llanfairfechan opening out below. Curve rightwards down the hillside now until the path takes you to a kissing gate in the wall. Go through the gate and bear half-right down the field to a ladder stile at the bottom of the slope. Follow an enclosed footpath to a ladder stile which takes you into a small field. Cross the field to enter a quiet lane.

Turn right along the lane and ignore the first turning on the left, instead, continue to the next junction where the footbridge can be crossed to return to the car park.

One of the Bronze Age standing stones which give Bwlch-y-Ddeufaen its name

Aber Falls

Distance: *6 miles*

A walk to one of North Wales' highest and most impressive waterfalls, hidden in the folds of the northern Carneddau. Return is made by a section of the North Wales Path, with wide views along the coast and across the Menai Strait to Anglesey. Footpaths are good throughout.

Start: Take the minor road which runs south from the A55 through Abergwyngregyn to the Aber Falls and park immediately before the bridge over Afon Aber ('Coedydd Aber Nature Reserve').
Grid ref: 663 720 (Landranger 115, Outdoor Leisure sheet 17).

The walk

1. Take the signed path to the Aber Falls which leaves the lane immediately before the bridge. This follows the right bank of the river at first before crossing a footbridge. Go through a kissing gate and turn right onto a broad obvious track. This track runs parallel to the river and takes you straight to the Aber Falls. (about 1³/₄ miles).

(An alternative path is signed to the left just before a small cottage—'Nant Rhaeadr'—which houses an exhibition open to the public between April and September. This path makes its way along the edge of the plantations on the left and could be used in conjunction with this path for a shorter circular walk.)

The falls can be seen for sometime on the approach—one of Wales' highest waterfalls. Afon Goch drains large areas of the northern

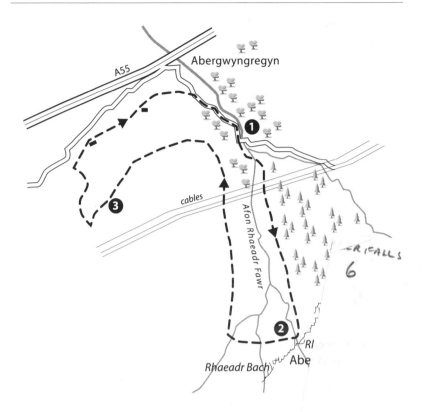

Carneddau and can be very impressive while in full
be viewed from directly below or from a grassy are

2. Cross the footbridge and bear right to a la
wall, signed for the 'North Wales Path' (I
obvious and well used path along the foot of
a second footbridge below Rhaeadr Bach—tl
waterfall'. Beyond this, turn right by a small pu_
North Wales Path sign (ignore a minor path on the left here) _
eventually run beside a ruined stone wall. Bear right through a
gap in the wall (indicated by the NWP sign) and continue to a
ladder stile beside a large gate which lies at the end of a farm
track. Follow the track which rises gradually up the hillside to
pass beneath a line of power cables.

There are excellent views from here, both back towards the Aber Falls at the head of the valley and the northern outliers of the Carneddau which back it, and to your right across the valley to Foel Ganol and the Roman road marked by pylons on the skyline. This road came up from ford at Tal-y-Cafn to Bwlch-y-Ddeufaen, then across the foot of Drum, Foel Ganol and down into the valley to Abergwyngregyn. The Roman leader Suetonius Paulinus used this route in AD 61 to reach Anglesey in a bid to put an end to the Druid resistance. This was successfully completed in one bloody massacre on the shores of the Menai Strait, when the Druid priests were slaughtered and their sacred groves burned to the ground. The road continued in use throughout the Roman period and became the main link between the forts at Caernarfon and Chester.

The Romans were, however, not the first to use this route through the mountains. The numerous prehistoric remains which line it testify to its antiquity and indicate that it had been in use throughout the Iron Age, Bronze Age and Neolithic period. The oak woods on the far side of the valley are remnants of the native woods which would have covered much of Snowdonia until the clearances of the Middle Ages.

Continue along the track until you pass a narrow wood on the left and broad views open out across the Lafan Sands to Anglesey. Ignore a footpath which bears right down to Abergwyngregyn (this path could be used to shorten the walk), instead, fork left (following NWP sign) onto a track which, after passing through a small wood, keeps to the top of the hillside.

The vast expanse of the Lafan Sands was used for many years as part of the route to Holyhead and Ireland. This may seem strange to us today, but prior to the building of coach roads in the late eighteenth century, most travel was carried out either on foot or horseback and where possible the shortest distance was taken. With no bridge at Menai until the 1820s, the shortest route from Conwy was across the Lafan Sands to Beaumaris and then through the centre of Anglesey to Holyhead by another tidal crossing to Holy Island. A ferry ran from Beaumaris to the edge of the sands for the crossing of the Menai Strait at low tide—one of the reasons why Beaumaris was previously such an important town on the island.

Aber Falls (Rhaeadr Fawr)

3. The track continues along the top of the hillside passing through a number of grazing fields. Immediately before the fourth ladder stile follow the track as it bends right and drops steeply down the field. Lower down the track curves right to a gate. Go through the gate and bear left off the track keeping close to the stream in the trees to your left. Look for a stile at the bottom of the field to the right of a small stone cottage. After the stile walk down the access road for about 20 yards or so before turning right through the centre of the field. Look for a ladder stile in the far fence beside a gate. Cut through the next field aiming for a stile behind farm buildings. At the end of the outbuildings drop to a gate which leads into the yard. Walk straight through the yard keeping the farmhouse on your left to enter fields again by a gate. Follow a track which runs across the field before rising to a gate and ladder stile. Beyond the gate the track contours the hillside.

At a fork, keep left and drop to a group of houses. Look for a ladder stile immediately to the left of the last house which leads into fields again. Walk directly through the field contouring the hillside and go through an iron kissing gate in the far corner. Keep to the field edge in the following field and pass through a second kissing gate. Bear half-right now following the obvious path and ignoring a ladder stile on the left adjacent to a house, which would take you into Abergwyngregyn. At the end of the path a kissing gate and steps take you into the lane. Turn right here and follow the lane back to the car park.

Llyn Geirionydd

Distance: 6¹/₂ *miles*

A walk over lower hillsides and through ancient woods to one of Snowdonia's most picturesque lakes. The locality is steeped in history and has links with both the Dark Age bard Taliesin and Prince Llywelyn. Paths are generally good with steeper ascents and descents near the start and end of the walk.

Start: There is limited parking along with WC facilities available in the centre of Trefriw opposite Trefriw Woollen Mill.

Grid ref: 780 630 (Landranger 115, Outdoor Leisure sheet 17)

The walk

1. With the woollen mill facing you, turn right over the bridge then left up the hill opposite the 'Fairy Falls Hotel'. Take the first footpath on the left in about 30 yards. Keep right where this path forks and walk beside the river to the Fairy Falls.

The falls were given their name by the Victorians who were fascinated by fairies and associated them with any romantic spot such as this.

From here the path bends sharp right up to a kissing gate. Go through the gate and turn right over the footbridge which crosses the rocky gorge containing the river. At a road cross over, go straight ahead and after a short rise, where the road bends left, follow a short footpath straight ahead.

At the top of the rise turn right along the road and look for a signed footpath which leads into woods on the left (approx 50 yards). This path rises gently for about 250 yards through the trees to a stile. After the stile in about 100 yards there is a fork, ignore the path on the left continuing ahead on the main path. This traverses the hillside with occasional glimpses of the valley through the trees.

Eventually you break out of the trees and you have a 'bird's eye view' into the valley. A little further on the path zig-zags up to an even better viewpoint. From here you can see you can see up the valley to the gap in the hills containing Llyn Crafnant with old mine buildings in the bottom of the valley.

Soon after this the path forks; ignore the path on the left, instead keep ahead on the more defined lower path which soon passes small walled fields on the left. Continue to contour crossing a stream by an old stone footbridge until you join the minor lane which runs beside Llyn Geirionydd (about ½ mile).

Keep right along the lane and turn right through the kissing gate at the start of the lake. Follow the track over the outflow and immediately after the first building on the left, turn left (post and sign) and follow a well defined path along the lake for about 1¼ miles. Just before this, a stone monument can be seen to the right of the track. If you visit the monument return to this point to continue the walk.

The monument was erected in 1850 by Lord Willoughby de Eresby of nearby Gwydir to commemorate the supposed birthplace of Taliesin, the famous sixth century bard. Numerous stories surround this mystical character but one of the best known is his association with King Maelgwyn Gwynedd. Maelgwyn, who ruled from AD 510-547, was the great-grandson of Cunedda, the powerful Celtic chieftain who came from one of the northern British kingdoms in the fifth century to rid Wales of Irish invaders and established the kingdom of Gwynedd. By the time of Maelgwyn, the Irish threat had gone and he was able to use a period of peace and prosperity to indulge in a life of extravagance and luxury rare at the time.

He built a palace at Deganwy on a hilltop known today as The Vardre, which overlooks the mouth of Afon Conwy, but his lifestyle soon brought condemnation and he was declared to be one of the most

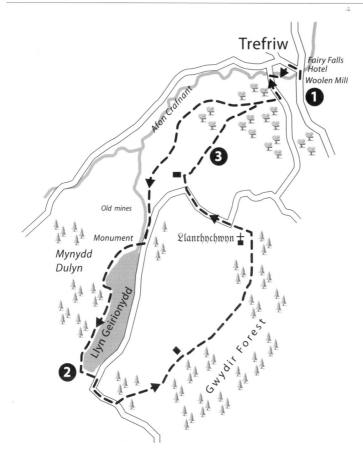

'sinful rulers' of his day by the monk Gildas, a sixth century chronicler and contemporary.

Despite his failings, Maelgwyn was a lover of music and poetry and harboured many musicians and bards at his court. On one occasion, his nephew Elffin came to visit and brought with him his bard, the great Taliesin. Maelgwyn's famous temper flared during the visit and the two parted enemies. Taliesin's parting gift to Maelgwyn was to foretell his death—"a creature would rise from Morfa Rhianedd (the plain on which Llandudno is now built) to punish him, 'its hair, its teeth and its eyes are yellow and this makes an end of Maelgwyn Gwynedd.'"

43

Llyn Geirionydd

Maelgwyn is said to have been so terrified that he locked himself into the church at Llanrhos but unable to resist his curiosity, he looked through the keyhole, saw the creature waiting and died on the spot.

The Taliesin Monument is also noted for its association with the Eisteddfod organised by the bard Gwilym Cowlyd (real name William John Roberts), in the second half of the nineteenth century. He worked as a poet, printer and bookseller and published the works of a number of fellow poets. As a bard he was highly respected and won the Chair at the National Eisteddfod at Conwy in 1861. His high standards led him into disagreement with the rules, so together with an associate, he organised a rival Eisteddfod in 1863 under the name of 'Arwest Glan Geirionydd'. The location was here around the Taliesin monument for obvious reasons and for a while it rivalled the National Eisteddfod in popularity, attracting entries from all over Wales.

When Gwilym died in 1904 at the age of 76, the great driving force behind the event was gone. It was held for the last time in 1912.

2. At the far end of the lake join a gravel track, turn left and continue to the lane. Turn right and follow the lane for about 500 yards to the first conifer plantation the left. Take the forest road on the left here and after 75 yards bear right onto a narrower footpath. This path eventually leads into fields by a stile. Bear half-left through the field to join an access track near spoil heaps on the left. Turn left here and follow the track to the right of the spoil heaps to a house. Pass through the garden of the house by two stiles (ignore a gate by conifers below on the right) and continue on the much fainter grass track rising to a large metal gate.

Go through the gate and walk straight ahead past a group of boulders to a stile in the fence on the right. Cross the stile and bear left through woods. A second stile in the fence on the left takes you out of the trees and along the woodland edge (for about 200 yards). The next stile takes you back into the trees again. In a few yards turn left onto a good footpath and follow this down the hillside past a number of old mine workings on the left.

At the bottom of the slope turn left onto a forest road and follow this to a farmhouse on the right. Immediately adjacent to the farmhouse, turn left up steps to a gate. At the top of the field go through a kissing gate and bear left up the field to another kissing gate in the wall. Turn left to visit Llanrhychwyn church.

This ancient church, reminiscent of the tiny church of St Celynin above Rowen, is said to be one of the oldest in Britain with parts of the building (about half its present form) dating back to the eleventh century, the time of Llywelyn ap Iorwerth (Llywelyn the Great). Traditionally, it is said to have been used by Llywelyn and his wife Princess Joan, daughter of King John, but in her later years Joan found the long walk so exhausting that Llywelyn had St Mary's church in Trefriw built for her convenience in 1230. The present form of the church dates from the eighteenth century, when a number of alterations were carried out.

From the church gate turn left to a kissing gate in the field corner and then right along the farm access road. At the T junction turn left, signposted 'Llyn Geirionydd'. Follow the lane for about 500 yards and, immediately after a gate across the road, turn right down a driveway lined with pine trees. Just before the house and garden turn right onto a track which soon bends left around the garden to a T junction with the house to the left. Turn right here, then right again at a second T junction. In about 75 yards, after the next gate, turn left through a second gate by sheep pens, then turn right up a sloping field. Keep close to the fence on the right and continue to a broad col at the top of the rise.

From this point, a short detour can be made by rising to the top of the rocky knoll on the left for a fine view of the surrounding countryside. Walkers are reminded that there is no right of way here.

The view takes in the Geirionydd and Crafnant valleys, with Moel Siabod peeping over the wooded slopes of Mynydd Deulyn. To the north, the hills plunge steeply into the Conwy Valley with the village of Trefriw at your feet.

3. Return to the col, go through a gate in the fence and turn left to a ladder stile over the far wall. This leads onto a path which drops steeply through the bracken. As the woods thicken, the path becomes less indistinct and curves right to join the well worn path used earlier. Turn right and retrace your route back to the Woolen Mill in the centre of Trefriw.

The name Trefriw is thought to mean 'healing town'—undoubtedly a reference to the mineral-rich waters which have been exploited here since Roman times.

Before the Industrial Revolution, Trefriw was a prominent trading centre and had the distinction of being the largest inland port in the whole of Wales. Goods were brought up the river by boat to a nearby quay and returned with slate, ore and timber from the hills above the village. It was also a centre for the local wool trade with the mill established to wash and finish cloth already woven by cottagers. This was known as a 'fulling' mill or Pandy.

Dolwyddelan

Distance: *6 miles*

A walk along a section of the Roman road known as Sarn Helen, into the hidden valley of Cwm Penamnen, with a link over the one of the enclosing hills to Castell Dolwyddelan, originally a fortress of the Welsh princes. Paths are generally good, with one steep section in the climb out of Cwm Penamnen.

Start: Free parking is available in the signed car park near Dolwyddelan railway station. Take the road opposite the Post Office in the centre of Dolwyddelan and the car park is on the left immediately after the bridge over Afon Lledr.

Grid ref: 737 521 (Landranger 115, Outdoor Leisure sheet 18).

The walk

1. Walk back to the road and turn left over the railway. Bear right immediately after the bridge and follow the road as it rises into the hidden valley of Cwm Penamnen (1½ miles).

This lane follows the line of the old Roman road which linked the forts of Caerhun in the Conwy Valley and Tomen-y-Muir near Trawsfynydd. Throughout the Dark Ages it continued to provide the main communication route with the south. The armies of the two Llywelyns, along with their famous ancestors, such as Owain Gwynedd and Gruffydd ap Cynan would all have marched this way to conflicts in South Wales and the southern borders.

Pass the track to 'Gwyndy', a farmhouse on the left and a little further on, immediately before a cottage on the left (Tan y Bwlch), take the signed footpath on the right. Climb steeply and directly up the hillside to a forest road. Opposite, the path continues to rise steeply through the trees. A stile at the end of the climb takes you onto the open hillside and you are treated to a grand view across the valley to the Moel Siabod, with the backs of the Glyderau and the Snowdon group to the left.

Follow the signed path ahead which heads directly down the hillside. Lower down (about ¾ mile), bear right along a more defined farm track. Remain on this track to a gate with a ruined farm building (about ¼ mile) to the right (possibly a 'hafod' or summer dwelling from earlier centuries). Ignore a path which bears to the right beside the ruin, instead go through the gate ahead and follow the track through grazing fields. After the next gate enter a smaller field with house roofs visible ahead (approx 200 yards away) and the castle on the far hillside. Shortly, take the signed footpath on the left (marked by small posts) to a ladder stile by a gate. Pass through a small field, then cross an old stone footbridge over the river. The path now keeps close to the river on the right to eventually meet the road. Turn right to the A470.

The present A470 over the Crimea Pass was only built in the mid-nineteenth century and received its name from the soldiers who built it who had recently returned from the Crimean War. The desolate moors between the Lledr Valley and Blaenau Ffestiniog evidently reminded them of the land in which they had fought and many of their comrades had died.

2. Cross the road and follow the lane opposite. This leads past Roman Bridge railway station, then over the railway and the river. Continue along the lane ignoring signed footpaths, first on the left, then on the right, until you reach a farm where the lane bends sharp left. Turn right here onto a signed footpath. At first you follow a track with gates and stiles then, where this bends left (about ¼ mile), bear right as indicated by a finger post onto a grassy path. Pass through a gate in a few yards then continue straight ahead on the obvious footpath.

Soon the castle comes into view and the path drops into a dip to join a concrete road to the left of, and a little beyond the castle.

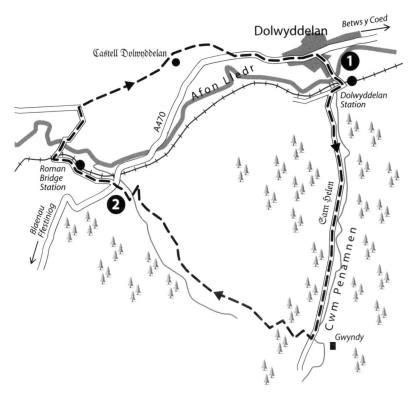

The castle is accessible by a path to the right but a fee is required to enter the keep where a small exhibition explains some of the castle's history. Tickets can be obtained by walking along the road a short distance to a path on the right which leads down to the ticket office.

Dolwyddelan is one of the few native Welsh castles from the period of the independent Princes still in existence. This is because the vast majority of castles built prior to the Edwardian Conquest were built from timber and have long since disappeared. In the case of Dolwyddelan, the original wooden structure, built about 1170 by Iorwerth Drwyndwn, Lord of Nant Conwy and father of Llywelyn the Great, was soon replaced by stone—an increasingly common practice among the Normans at that time. Llywelyn is thought to have been born here in 1173 but was removed as an infant for safe upbringing in Powys, the land of his mother, when his father was killed. When he returned to take control of the Kingdom of Gwynedd in 1195, Dolwyddelan became one of his main strongholds and he has many associations with both the Lledr and Conwy valleys.

The castle was used extensively throughout the thirteenth century by both Llywelyn the Great and his grandson, sometimes referred to as 'Llywelyn the Last' (being the last independent Welsh prince) in their wars with both the English kings and Welsh rivals, often from within their own families. Dolwyddelan finally fell to the armies of Edward I in 1283 after a two month winter siege following the death of Llywelyn at Builth Wells. Although there were a few minor battles still to be fought, the fall of Dolwyddelan is generally accepted as signalling the end of Welsh resistance to Edward I.

Castell Dolwyddelan

The present structure dates from the fifteenth century when an extra floor was added giving the tower is square top and battlements. In 1489 the castle was acquired by Maredudd ab Ieuan, an ancestor of the Wynns of Gwydir. The name Wynn was derived from Ieuan in Tudor times when the English fashion for surnames was being followed by the Welsh gentry. Maredudd is said to have been responsible for the building of St Gwyddelon's church in Dolwyddelan to replace an earlier church with the same dedication. The new church was said to have been more visible from Maredudd's new house in Cwm Penamnen and more easily defended. The reason for this precaution seems to have been the nearby hospice of Ysbyty Ifan. This was an area of sanctuary run by the Knights of the Order of St John of Jerusalem over which the king's officials had no authority or right of entry. Over the centuries it had attracted all manor of outlaws and undesirables who began to prey on the surrounding areas. Maredudd thus felt vulnerable in his mountain valley and he is said to have attended church accompanied by a small army.

It may have been for this reason that Maredudd bought and moved to Gwydir near Llanrwst in the Conwy Valley in 1500. His son, John Wynn, was the first to use the name which was to become synonymous, not just with Gwydir, but most of the Conwy Valley. In the nineteenth century the ruins of Dolwyddelan were renovated by Lord Willoughby de Eresby, a descendant of Maredudd ab Ieuan.

Continue along the road to the A470 (ignoring a road which curves to the right). Turn left and return to Dolwyddelan where a right turn at the Post Office will take you back to the car park.

The Lledr Valley

Distance: *6½ miles*

A wooded riverside walk along a peaceful stretch on Afon Lledr followed by a steep rise to the medieval house of Ty Nant in its remote valley. Return is made by forestry tracks and open hillsides. Can be boggy under foot during wet periods but footpaths are generally good.

Start: As for the previous route.

Grid ref: 737 521 (Landranger 115, Outdoor Leisure sheet 18).

The walk

1. Turn right out of the car park opposite the school and walk along the lane. After a farm the lane deteriorates into a track and a little further on you pass a footbridge on the left over the river. Don't cross the river, instead keep ahead along the track which eventually passes under the railway again. Bear left after the railway and continue to join a lane after houses.

This lane and the path which we have been following beside the railway is thought to have been part of the Roman road known as Sarn Helen. It came over from Pentre-Du near Betws-y-Coed and continued to Dolwyddelan, then turned south climbing into Cwm Penamnen. It linked the Roman camps at Caerhun in the Conwy Valley and Tomen-y-Muir near Trawsfynydd.

Walk along the lane passing the railway station and where the lane eventually bends left over the bridge to join the main road (A470), keep ahead past 'Plas Hall Hotel'. Where the lane shortly turns right to 'Lledr Hall Outdoor Education Centre', take the enclosed footpath straight ahead. Keep straight ahead at a driveway and in a few yards bear left onto a stone flagged path towards the river (ignore a path on the right which leads towards the railway). The path is now well used and obvious and runs beside Afon Lledr (approx 1/2 mile).

After passing through two gates about 50 yards apart, turn left immediately and follow a beautiful wooded section of the river as it runs through a rocky gorge.

After the woods, the path stays close to the river with fields on the right. At a farmhouse, turn left down the drive and immediately before the bridge turn right over a stile and walk through a campsite beside the river.

After the campsite a stile in the fence takes you into woods again. In a few yards the path forks—keep straight ahead here ignoring the path to the left. At the railway viaduct (Pont Gethin), turn right through the arch (stile). Immediately there is a ladder stile over the fence on the right. Go over this stile and bear left to pick up a path which is faint for the first few yards then becomes better established. At a T junction turn left and follow this path to a lane.

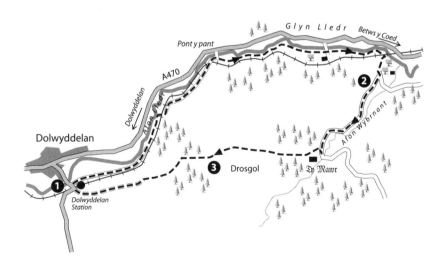

Ty Mawr Wybrnant

2. Turn right and follow the rising lane for about ¹/₂ mile to the hidden cwm of Wybrnant. Here the angles eases and the lane runs beside Afon Wybrnant which tumbles through rocks to your left. Continue along the lane to the restored period house of Ty Mawr, managed by the National Trust.

Ty Mawr is the birth place of Bishop William Morgan, who produced the first Welsh translation of the Bible. He was born here in the early 1540s and went to Cambridge in 1565 where he studied eight languages including the Hebrew, Latin and Greek which he was to use in his translation work. He entered the church in 1568 becoming the Bishop of Llandaf and later St. Asaph.

Most of his work on the Welsh Bible is said to have been carried out at Llanrhaeadr-ym-Mochnant near the English border. It also included the work of William Salesbury who had translated much of the New Testament into Welsh and who is thought to have been a friend, or at least an associate of William Morgan. His work was published in 1588 under the title 'Y Beibl Cyssegr-Lan'—'The Holy Bible'. The cost of publication was born by John Whitgift, Archbishop of Canterbury and was dedicated to Queen Elizabeth I whose ancestors, through Henry Tudor, came from Gwynedd. Morgan died in 1604.

Ty Mawr is open to the public and visitors can see just how basic life was even for those of reasonable means during this period.

From Ty Mawr walk back along the lane for about 100 yards and take the signed footpath on the left immediately after a gate across the lane. After a gate, turn left along the wall and eventually enter felled woodland by a stile. Take the obvious path through the trees and at a forest track turn right, then immediately left onto a faint path. Continue to rise between old stone walls and at the next forest track, cross over keeping straight ahead again. Follow the path through an area of recently felled trees to a ladder stile in the fence. The next section of path is easy to follow but can be very wet in parts.

There are superb views of the Snowdon group and Moel Siabod across the valley to the right. The flat topped hills to the right of Siabod are the Carneddau and there is a brief glimpse of Tryfan's serrated profile over the shoulder of Siabod shortly after crossing the stile.

3. After about ½ mile a stile takes you into conifer woods again and a well used path descends through the trees.

About 50 yards before fields on the left, bear left off the path onto what is initially a less obvious path. This soon runs close to the fenced field on the right where you will be able to enjoy a view down to Dolwyddelan and up the valley to the Snowdon group.

At the end of the fenced field cotinue ahead on a good path through the trees and descending gently. Pass quarries on the right and go between two stone pillars. A straight path down one of the old inclines leads to a forest road. Turn left and follow the road to Dolwyddelan. Turn right by houses and cross the railway to return to the car park

Roman Bridge

Distance: *6¹/₂ or 7³/₄ miles*

A walk to a superb viewpoint and isolated lake using forest tracks and open moorland paths in a little known walking area at the head of Glyn Lledr. Footpaths are indistinct in parts and sections can be very wet under foot in poor weather. In very wet weather there may be problems crossing a stream in the early part of the walk.

Start: Begin the walk in the narrow lane which leads past Roman Bridge Station at the head of the Lledr Valley. This is situated on the north side of the A470 approximately 2 miles west of Dolwyddelan. It is possible to park just after the bridge over the river (past the station and railway) where the lane widens for a short section.

Grid ref: 711 516 (Landranger 116, Outdoor Leisure sheets 17 & 18).

The walk

1. If you have parked beyond the bridge over the river, walk back towards it and a few yards short, turn right onto a signed field path. This field is often wet or marshy, but the path is paved with large flat stones and soon turns left. Cross a stream by a footbridge tucked under the hedge and continue through the following fields with the river close by on the left at first, before it veers away and the path makes a gentle rise through two more fields to reach a quiet lane. Turn left along the lane for about 100 yards before turning right through the gate to 'Fridd'. Keep the house to your right and go through a large gate straight ahead which leads onto a farm track.

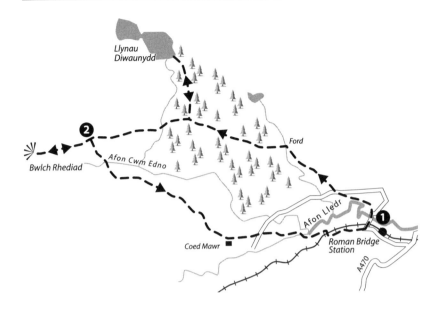

The track rises gently for about 600 yards before turning sharp right. Continue straight ahead here following a narrower but still well defined footpath which leads, in about 300 yards, to a ford across the stream. Cross the stream and a stile which takes you into conifer plantations. Under normal conditions there is no problem here, large stepping stones make the crossing easy, but during or immediately after heavy rain it may difficult to cross the stream here.

Follow the obvious path through the conifers for about ¾ mile. The path rises steadily and is signed frequently with yellow waymarks. Cross two forest roads continuing straight ahead each time unless you want to make the detour (¾ mile each way) to Llynau Diwaunydd. These twin lakes lie in an isolated cwm and make a make an ideal place for a break. For this option turn right at the second forest road. Return to this point to continue the walk turning right at the waymarked post.

A muddy path leads to a ladder stile which takes you out of the plantations and onto the open moors. The path continues straight ahead contouring the hillside and rising very slightly (marked by wooden posts). The correct path passes above ruined sheep enclosures down to the left and aims for the right-hand side of a small group of conifers ahead. The conical peak ahead is Yr Aran, one of Snowdon's satellite peaks.

2. When you reach the conifers you have another choice; you can either turn left to make your return on the south side of the valley or continue for another ¾ mile to Bwlch y Rhediad where you will be treated to superb views of the Snowdon Horseshoe and Llyn Gwynant in clear conditions. If you take this option, return to this point to continue the walk.

As you approach the pass the conical peak of Yr Aran, which has been visible for sometime on your walk across the moor, is suddenly joined by the peaks of Y Lliwedd, Y Wyddfa (Snowdon) and Crib Goch, which have been hidden behind the crags of Clogwyn Pwll Budr until now. Beyond Yr Aran is Moel Hebog, rising above the wooded hillsides and green fields of Nantgwynant.

This pass undoubtedly provided an important communication route in past centuries linking communities in Nantgwynant, Glyn Lledr and Dyffryn Conwy. It avoided the long haul to Pen y Gwryd and the difficult negotiation of the Llugwy gorge between Capel Curig and Betws-y-Coed. As such, it may also have provided an important route to the east from the western side of Snowdonia throughout the Middle Ages and even earlier. The existence of stone paving, apparent in the early stages of the walk and at several points during the forest section, along with the name Sarn Diwaunydd, may also be an indication that this path was used as a road in earlier times.

From the pass return to the small group of conifers passed earlier and after crossing two streams beyond a small ruin (about 150 yards), turn right and head for a footbridge over Afon Cwm Edno. Walk up to a stile and then continue the rise to a track. Turn left here and follow the track for about 1¼ miles with broad views to the left of Moel Siabod rising above the conifer woods visited earlier with Snowdon and Y Lliwedd behind.

As you approach the farm of Coed Mawr, bear left between outbuildings to join a lane. Follow the lane down to a T junction in the bottom of the valley with a house to the left. Take the signed footpath opposite walking diagonally across the field to a small gate in the corner. Go through the gate and walk in the same direction keeping to the right of a small fenced quarry. At the end of the fence bear right and walk along the river to a footbridge on the right. Cross the footbridge and a stile, then bear half-left across a small field to an access track. Turn left and follow the access track over the river and railway. Continue along the track passing through a farmyard to reach the lane used earlier. Turn either right or left here depending on where you parked.

Yr Aran, Moel Hebog and Llyn Gwynant from Bwlch y Rhediad

The Llugwy Valley

Distance: 6½ miles

An exploration of the wooded hillsides either side of Afon Llugwy between Capel Curig and Betws-y-Coed. There are well known beauty spots along the way as well as lesser known corners. Paths and forest tracks are excellent throughout.

Start: Begin the walk at Pont-y-Pair, the old stone bridge which carries the B5106 over Afon Llugwy in the centre of Betws-y-Coed *Grid ref: 791 567*. Parking is available in a number of car parks throughout the village. For a shorter round, begin at the forest car park on the A5 'Caen-y-Coed', mid way between the Swallow Falls and The Ugly House (Ty Hyll) *Grid ref: 762 576*. *(Landranger 115, Outdoor Leisure sheet 17).*

The walk

1. From the A5 in the centre of Betws-y-Coed cross the river and take the first road on the left immediately after the bridge. In about 30 yards there is a pay and display car park on your right— bear left here and follow the riverside footpath, for about ¾ mile.

As the river narrows and its banks become more wooded, a small gorge is entered and a wooden footbridge known as the 'Miner's Bridge' spans the river.

The 'Miner's Bridge', along with the nearby 'Miner's Arms' recalls the occupation of many locals when lead mining was carried out in the numerous mines of the Gwydir Forest during the nineteenth century. The original bridge provided a short-cut for miners living at Pentre Du on the south side of the river saving them the mile and a half walk via the old bridge at Betws-y-Coed. The bridge is also the approximate

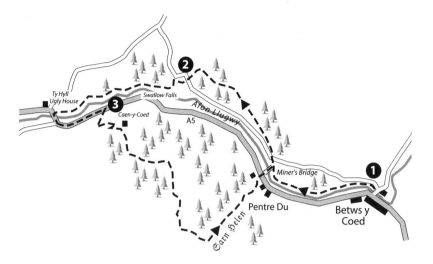

location of the crossing made by Sarn Helen, the Roman road which linked the forts of Caerhun, in the Conwy Valley, with the larger camp at Tomen-y-Muir, near Trawsfynydd to the south.

Do not cross the Miner's Bridge, instead bear right up the hillside to a lane. Follow the signed footpath opposite. This well used and obvious footpath runs diagonally up the hillside with a hint of the deepening valley to your left through the trees.

At the top of the rise a stile leads into fields. Take the path directly ahead passing a small farm on the left. At the farm access track, turn left along the track towards the farm. About 30 yards before the farm gate turn right and walk through the centre of the field (tree) following the faint line of a track in the grass. At a gate and stile, enter woods and take the lower (straight ahead) and more obvious of the two paths down through the trees. Shortly you emerge from the trees with fields on the left and a fine view of the wooded Llugwy Valley to Moel Siabod on the skyline.

Keep beside the wall until a gate at the end of the path leads into fields. Do not go through the gate, instead bear right along the wall following a vague path until you meet a faint path coming down from the right. Turn left here and walk down through the trees with fields to the left, to a stile which leads into a small field. Cross a second stile after a few yards and pass beside a garden to enter a lane.

2. Turn left and walk along the lane for about 50 yards before turning sharp right onto a path. After stone steps turn left, then a little further on, turn right onto a good path which soon crosses a footbridge over a stream. Follow the signed path to the left after the bridge and eventually meet a forest track. Bear right along this track for about 30 yards before leaving it again for a path on the left (yellow markers on trees).

Stay on this path for about 600 yards ignoring paths on the right. Eventually you enter the narrow gorge high above Afon Llugwy with good views of the Swallow Falls from the little viewing area.

The Swallow Falls

The Swallow Falls are probably the most famous falls in North Wales although they are neither the highest nor the most spectacular. Their popularity has its origins in the establishment of Betws-y-Coed as a tourist destination during the nineteenth century. The original name of the falls was Rhaeadr Ewynnol, which means 'foaming falls'. This name seems to have been mistaken by the Victorians for the similar word, Rhaeadr-y-Wennol, which means 'swallow falls' and the name has remained.

The mistreated tenants of the infamous Sir John Wynn of Gwydir, who owned much of the surrounding land, comforted themselves after his death in the belief that his soul had been condemned to remain for ever beneath these foaming waters as punishment for his crimes against them.

Beyond the falls a good path stays close to the river for about ¹/₂ mile to reach the A5 at Ty Hyll, more popularly known as the 'Ugly House'.

The Ugly House, said to date from the fourteenth century, is another one the area's tourist attractions and decorates numerous old postcards and calendars from earlier decades of the twentieth century. It is said to be the result of a local law which stated that if a house could be built between sunset and sunrise the builders owned the house and the land it was built on. The promoters of this tale evidently paid little attention to the impossibility of moving such huge boulders into place in a single night!

Turn left over the bridge and walk along the road for just under ¹/₂ mile to the forest car park (Caen-y-Coed) on the right.

3. Turn right here and take the forest road which rises sharply to the right. Where this bends back to the left, bear right onto a long straight forest road which rises steadily through the trees. Near the top of the rise, bear left onto a narrower gravel track which continues the climb to a gate and cattle grid leading into fields. Go through the gate and follow the track to a small farm. Enter the farmyard and bear right to a gate adjacent to the farmhouse. Go through this and follow the rising grass track behind the farm. At the top of the rise pass through a gate near barns and continue on the faint track to a stile and gate which lead onto a forest road. Turn left here and follow this road as it contours round the hillside ignoring paths and tracks on the right. Keep right where a track joins from the left and continue for almost ¹/₂ mile to where the track forks. Bear right here and after about 300 yards, opposite a lane on the right, turn left onto a descending path/track between stone walls.

This path is part of an ancient road over the hills known as Sarn Helen. It was formalised by the Romans and was part of the link between the forts of Caerhun in the Conwy Valley and Tomen-y-Muir near Trawsfynydd. The Romans often formalised existing routes and tracks, particularly in difficult terrain. This route over the hills may well have been in use for many centuries before the Romans came here.

At a forest road with a cottage on the right, continue the descent straight ahead to emerge in the settlement of Pentre Du. Cross the A5 and take the path opposite down to the Miner's Bridge. Cross the bridge, turn right and follow the riverside path back to Betws-y-Coed.

Snowdon from Deiniolen (route 13)

Yr Aran from Beddgelert Forest (route 16)

Llyn Idwal from below the Devil's Kitchen (route 10)

Llyn Cwellyn (route 17)

Snowdon from Llynnau Mymbyr (route 8)

Snowdon and Crib Goch from Capel Curig (route 8)

Snowdon from Llyn Padarn (route 13)

Snowdon from (route 14)

Tryfan and the Glyderau seen across the woods of Gwydir

Moel Siabod from the Gwydir Forest (route 11)

Snowdon from above Capel Curig (routes 8 & 11)

The East Face of Tryfan (route 9)

Dolwyddelan with the Snowdon group in the distance (route 4)

Cloud on the Glyder range from Nant Ffrancon (route 12)

Llyn Crafnant (route 11)

Yr Aran from Llyn Gwynant (route 14)

Capel Curig

Distance: *4¹/₄ miles*

A short easy walk on the low hillsides above Capel Curig and beside Afon Llugwy. The walk visits two of the most famous viewpoints in Snowdonia: the Snowdon Horseshoe from the Capel Curig Pinnacles and the shore of Llynnau Mymbyr.

Start: Begin the walk from the car park situated behind the shops in Capel Curig.

Grid ref: 720 581   (Landranger 115, Outdoor Leisure sheet 17).

The walk

1. Turn left out of the car park and walk over the old bridge to join the road with shops to your left. Turn half-left, cross the A5 and take the signed footpath directly opposite. This rises through grazing fields towards a small rocky peak which overlooks Capel Curig and gives a classic view of the Snowdon group rising beyond Llynnau Mymbyr. The path passes to the left of the rocks eventually entering woods by a stile or gate. Follow the well worn footpath ahead through the trees, then across the bracken covered hillside below Clogwyn Mawr. Climb over a ladder stile and continue to a gap in a ruined stone wall. Bear right off the main path here to a stone footbridge over the stream and make your way rightwards crossing a second smaller footbridge to pass the gate of a cottage on the left.

A small grass platform adjacent to the gate gives a classic view down the valley to the Snowdon group with the backs of the Glyderau to the right and the tree covered slopes of Moel Siabod falling to the 'twin lakes' of Llynnau Mymbyr on the left.

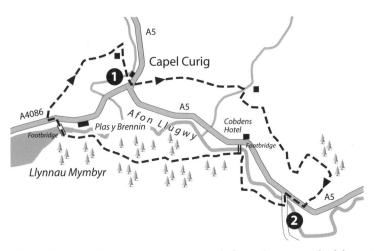

Keep beside the garden on your left and cross a ladder stile lower down. Keep left by the fence again, turning left onto a faint grass track. This leads in a few yards to a gate onto a rough access road beside 'Bryn Tyrch Uchaf'. Bear left along a track for a few yards, then left again to follow a path beside the fence on your left. Pass above an old wooden chalet to reach a ladder stile. Beyond the stile continue straight ahead through a gap in a wall of large boulders, over a track and ahead down to a ladder stile leading into woods. Follow the well worn footpath through the trees ignoring a path to the right lower down.

Pass a small stone building on the left and a little further on meet a rising track. Turn left up the hill and after a bend (right then left) and a gap in a stone wall look for an obvious path on the right. Follow this path with good views both into and along the valley and across to Moel Siabod. At a small cottage on the left turn right down the hill to a stile which leads to a car park.

2. Walk through the car park and turn right along the main road (A5). Shortly, turn left over the old stone bridge and take the signed footpath on the right almost immediately, which follows an access road for a few yards before bearing right down the bank. Cross the footbridge and follow the riverside footpath to the left.

In the corner of the last field, a ladder stile takes you into woods. Shortly, an obvious path bears left away from the river (the riverside footpath continues ahead to a footbridge) and leads up a tiny 'valley' or depression. Follow this footpath and at the top of the slope, join the path which rises from the right. Turn left through 'slits' in the rock and follow the path with the river and the A5 down to your right.

The path soon develops into a forest road. Continue to a T junction. Turn left here, then bear right shortly at a fork and follow the forest road to 'Bryn Engan', a large house on the right. Go through the gate straight ahead and continue to the footbridge at Plas-y-Brenin (meaning 'King's Palace' or 'Hall) Outdoor Education Centre.

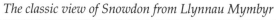

The classic view of Snowdon from Llynnau Mymbyr

Plas-y-Brenin is now a well established outdoor pursuits centre but was originally built as a sixty-room hotel during the first decade of the nineteenth century when it was known as 'The Royal Hotel'. It was built by Lord Penrhyn who owned the Penrhyn slate quarries at Bethesda and who was responsible for building the first coach road through the Ogwen Valley between 1791 and 1800, where previously there had only been a packhorse trail. By 1803 the Capel Curig Turnpike Trust had built a link road from Capel Curig through Betws-y-Coed to Pentrefoelas, and London to Holyhead coaches immediately began to use this instead of the longer and more hazardous alternative through Conwy and along the coast. The hotel would thus have originally catered for those travelling between London and Ireland.

In 1815 Thomas Telford was commissioned to improve the entire London to Holyhead road as several sections had gradients of 1 in 6 which meant difficult and dangerous travelling for coaches (second class travellers were obliged to get out and push on the steeper sections). For the most part, he followed the same line as the existing route through the mountains, passing through both Betws-y-Coed and Capel Curig. The Irish mail coaches used this route regularly until the building of the railways. By then, however, both Capel Curig and Betws-y-Coed had been placed firmly on the tourist map and have continued to cater for tourists ever since.

Cross the footbridge and rise to the road. Turn left and after 150 yards or so turn right over a ladder stile. The path bears half-left from the stile for about 20 yards, before two tracks curve right. Follow the second track which contours the hillside to join Lord Penrhyn's road after a cottage on the right. Turn right here and return to Capel Curig.

Llyn Cowlyd from Capel Curig

Distance: *7¹/₄ or 9 miles*

A walk accross the open, lower slopes of the eastern Carneddau with the option to take in two of the lower tops. Excellent mountain views in clear conditions. Footpaths are good but some sections can be very boggy in wet conditions. Lightweight footware not reccommended.

Start: As for the previous route.

Grid ref: 720 581   (Landranger 115, Outdoor Leisure sheet 17).

The walk

1. Turn left out of the car park and walk over the old bridge to join the road with shops to your left. Turn left and walk along the A5 for about ¹/₂ mile.

About 100 yards beyond a house on the right turn right onto a signed footpath. Walk diagonally-left up the gentle hillside, initially following a line of power cables before they veer away to the left. Quite soon the buttresses of Tryfan's East Face come into view over the shoulder of Galt yr Ogof to the left.

The path is well used and easy to follow (although often wet). Pass a small stone farmhouse on the left and continue ahead to a ladder stile beside an old iron gate. Bear right after the stile and follow the well worn footpath across the open moors with the cone of Pen Llithrig-y-Wrach directly ahead and widening views of the Ogwen Valley to the left.

The view along the valley to the left is dominated by the buttresses of Tryfan and the fangs of Bristly Ridge on Glyder Fach, with the more rounded slopes of the Carneddau falling away to the right. Beyond Ogwen, the chiselled face of Foel Goch and the enclosing arms of Y Garn become visible from behind Tryfan.

Higher up you cross one of the leats which channel water from the southern slopes of the Carneddau into the Llyn Cowlyd Reservoir. Further on, a large footbridge leads over the inflow to the lake—the deepest in Snowdonia—which can be seen to the right. Cross the bridge.

2. The path splits three ways here—the trail to the right follows the northern shore of Llyn Cowlyd; the path to the summit of Pen Llithrig-y-Wrach begins its climb here and a third path turns to the left.

For the shortest and least strenuous walk, turn left beside the fence. Shortly there is a stile in the fence on the left. Turn left over the stile and go ahead to cross the leat again. Turn right immediately onto the well-used path which runs beside the leat. Continue on this path with superb views in clear weather towards Tryfan and Glyder Fach. At the second bridge over the leat (not counting the one you crossed) you will see an obvious path on the left which makes its way across the open moors towards Tryfan (in clear conditions) and a small farm lower down in the distance. Turn left onto this path.

Lower down the path becomes less obvious and the farm disappears but its position is maked by a group of trees which remain visible. Continue towards the trees soon running beside the stream (Afon Bedol). At a stone footbridge turn right, cross the bridge and go ahead through a gateway. Walk ahead beside the wall on the left towards a stone building on the skyline. Pass the building continuing beside the wall to a gate in the wall on the left above a farm lower down the hillside (just before walled sheep pens). Turn left through the gate and walk down towards

The East Face of Tryfan remains visible for much of the walk

Tryfan and the Ogwen Valley from the east

the farm. About halfway towards the farm turn right over a small footbridge, then bear left down past the farm to the access track. Turn right down the track to the A5. Continue from point 3.

Alternatively, from the bridge over the inflow to Llyn Cowlyd (point 2) you can extend the walk to include the tops of Pen Llithrig-y-Wrach and Pen yr Helgi Du, by taking the path directly ahead after the bridge. The path zig-zags steeply up through rocks and heather to the summit.

From the summit some of the finest views in Snowdonia can be enjoyed. Northwards the panorama takes in Llandudno, Conwy and much of the Conwy Valley backed by the Denbigh Moors. Nearer at hand lie the broad glacial valleys holding Llyn Eigiau and the Llyn Cowlyd Reservoir which drain the eastern slopes of the Carneddau. Across the Ogwen Valley stand the more rugged outlines of Tryfan and the Glyderau with the serrated ridges of Y Gribin and Bristly Ridge seen in profile. The summit of Snowdon can just be seen, along with Y Lliwedd's triple peak over the shoulder of Galt yr Ogof.

To the south lies the unmistakable bulk of Moel Siabod with the Moelwynion beyond. On the farthest skyline lie the peaks of southern Snowdonia, with the Berwyn hills and Clwydian Range to the east.

Cwm Eigiau is one of the major valleys on this part of the Carneddau and its glacial origin, giving it the classic 'U' shape, can be clearly seen from here.

Follow the west ridge to the summit of Pen yr Helgi Du, then turn due south and walk down the broad ridge of Y Braich to the stile which leads onto the leat at the foot of the ridge. Cross the stile by the bridge and bear half-right onto a faint grass path with Glyder Fach and Bristly Ridge directly ahead. The path soon disappears (ignore a more prominent contouring path which heads off in the direction of Tryfan) but it is not difficult to keep on the same diagonal descent line (towards a farm in the base of the valley) until a farm comes into view on the left and sheep pens ahead. Keep to the right of the sheep pens where a prominent ladder stile leads over the wall. Keep in the same direction (towards a small group of pines down on the A5) until a farm track is reached. Turn right and follow the track to the road.

3. Cross the A5 and climb the ladder stile directly opposite. Take the obvious path through a boulder strewn field towards a group of Scots pines. A ladder stile leads onto a broad path here which is all that now remains of the old road built by Lord Penrhyn. Turn left and follow the old road back to Capel Curig (about 2 miles).

Until 1790 there was no road through the Ogwen Valley; the only route being a rough packhorse trail used occasionally by drovers. It was only with the improvements carried out by Richard Pennant during the 1790s that a road capable of carrying wheeled traffic was built. Part of his road is still in use on the west side of Nant Ffrancon below Llyn Ogwen, the extension to Capel Curig (the path we are now following), where he built what is now Plas Y Brenin outdoor Education Centre, (then 'The Royal Hotel') was not used once Thomas Telford built what is now the A5.

Llyn Idwal &
The Devil's Kitchen

Distance: *5¹/₂ miles*

A rough rugged walk visiting two beautiful lakes situated in the heart of the mountains. In clear conditions the mountain scenery is amongst the most spectacular in Snowdonia. Although footpaths are reasonable throughout, this is one of the roughest walks in the book and shouldn't be attempted in lightweight footware. The route is best avoided in poor weather.

Start: Parking is available in a large layby at the eastern end of Llyn Ogwen on the A5.

Grid ref. 666 605 (Landranger 115, Outdoor Leisure sheet 17).

The walk

1. From the layby cross the river by the stone bridge and pass through a small group of pines. Pass 'Glan Denna' on the left and continue over the cattle grid on the farm track towards 'Tal-y-Llyn Ogwen' farm.

Just before the farm turn right on the signed path beside the wall. At a stile on the left cross the wall. The well-made path to Cwm Ffynnon Lloer bends right up beside the stream here. Don't take this path, keep straight ahead on a less distinct path (directly towards Y Garn) passing above the farm to cross a stream by a footbridge. From here the path continues ahead on a contouring line with Llyn Ogwen down to your left.

This path gives excellent views of Tryfan, the Glyderau and the

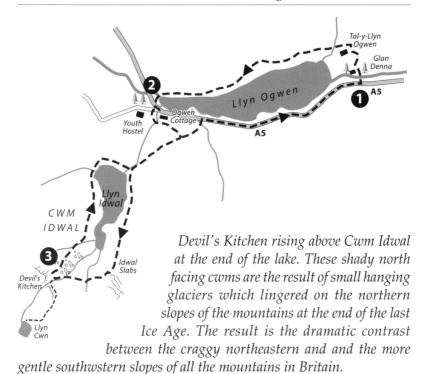

Devil's Kitchen rising above Cwm Idwal at the end of the lake. These shady north facing cwms are the result of small hanging glaciers which lingered on the northern slopes of the mountains at the end of the last Ice Age. The result is the dramatic contrast between the craggy northeastern and and the more gentle southwstern slopes of all the mountains in Britain.

Partway along the path there is an area of easy angled slabs which tumble down towards the lake shore. These slabs have been polished smooth by the belly of a massive glacier which would have filled the entire valley to a depth of perhaps 500 metres or more during the last Ice Age. This glacier is thought to have been one of numerous 'tongues' of ice forced through the mountains by the weight of an enormous ice cap situated to the east. These 'tongues' or 'fingers' of ice are also resposible for the present form of valleys such as nearby Nant Ffrancon, the Llanberis Pass, Nant Gwynant and the Conwy Valley.

Beyond the slabs the path continues, gradually dropping, to eventually run close to the shore of the lake.

2. Near the end of the lake make your way through an area of huge boulders to the reach the road (A5). Turn left and walk along the road to Ogwen Cottage (Outdoor Pursuits Centre, Mountain Rescue Post and Youth Hostel). Turn right into the car

Llyn Idwal and Cwm Idwal with the Devil's Kitchen and the Idwal slabs

park (toilets and snack bar) then bear left onto the Llyn Idwal path immediately before the toilets.

The path is well used and after crossing the stream heads towards the bwlch between Tryfan and Glyder Fach before reaching a fork. Keep right with the main path soon reaching the northern shore of Llyn Idwal.

You will have been aware of the dark brooding cliffs at the head of the lake and the huge cleft known as the 'Devil's Kitchen', for some time on the approach, but as you reach the lake the whole dramatic scene opens out. Despite being one of the wildest and most impressive cwms in Snowdonia, Cwm Idwal is probably one of the most accessible.

It was here in Cwm Idwal that the glacial origin of much of our highland landscape was first discovered. This discovery was made by

Charles Darwin, best known for his theories on evolution, but Darwin was in fact a geologist rather than a biologist and made several visits to Cwm Idwal to study the unique landscape and its rock structure.

The rocks of the cwm are mainly volcanic, thought to be 450 million years old and are distorted into a huge 'U' shaped fold—known as the 'Idwal Syncline'—which can be seen in rock layers forming the distinctive terraces which curve upwards on either side of the Devil's Kitchen. The present form of the cwm however, owes its existence to much more recent events—the action of ice during the last Ice Age. Evidence suggests that at its greatest extent ice spilled over from above the Devil's Kitchen and flowed down into the cwm in the form of an ice tongue up to 1,500 feet thick which then joined the main Ogwen/Nant Ffrancon glacier, possibly deflecting the latter and causing it to turn through almost 90 degrees. The result—Nant Ffrancon—is one of the most spectacular legacies from the Ice Age in Wales. As the ice dwindled

Looking across to Pen-yr-Ole Wen from Ogwen Cottage

it left behind the mounds of debris known as 'moraines' which can be seen on the far side of the lake and are passed later in the walk.

Follow the path ahead along the eastern shore passing the foot of the Idwal Slabs which form the northern face of Glyder Fawr. From here the path steepens to pass through the chaos of enormous boulders torn from the cliffs above. Follow this path to a junction (not all that obvious) near a group of particularly large boulders and with the Devil's Kitchen almost directly above.

3. From here a path continues to climb to the foot of the Devil's Kitchen, then bears left along one of the wide rocky terraces to reach to top of the crags. There is no difficulty on this path other than that already encountered climbing over bouders, but it is strenuous. At the top there are grand views back into Cwm Idwal and over to Snowdon. There is also a small lake—Llyn Cwn— an excellnt picnic spot in good weather. From here return to the path junction in the boulder field and bear left.

Alternatively, you can miss out the climb to the top by turning right at the junction by the group of large boulders and following the descending path down to the western shore of Llyn Idwal passing between the moraine ridges mentioned earlier. Continue to the end of the lake.

Turn right along the shingle shore and cross the footbridge over the outflow to reach path used earlier. Turn left and head back towards Ogwen Cottage. Where the path swings sharp left bear right—not onto the most obvious path which climbs up towards Tryfan and Glyder Fach, but a little to the left of this where a faint path takes a diagonal line down towards the road. A number of stiles cross the wall to reach the road. Turn right along the road to complete the walk.

Llyn Crafnant & the Gwydir Forest

Distance: *7¹/₂ miles*

An excellent walk with some superb views of Snowdon and Moel Siabod. The well-used and popular path from Capel Curig to Llyn Crafnant is followed by the forest roads and paths of the Gwydir Forest. Footpaths and forest tracks are good throughout.

Start: Begin the walk from the little car park situated behind the shops in Capel Curig.

Grid ref: 720 581 (Landranger 115, Outdoor Leisure sheet 17).

The walk

1. Turn left out of the car park and walk over the old bridge to join the road with shops to your left. Turn left, cross the A5 and take the signed footpath directly opposite beside the old church. This rises through a grazing field towards the little rocky peak known as Capel Curig Pinnacles. (It is worth the short detour to the top of the Pinnacles for the classic view of the Snowdon group rising from beyond Llynnau Mymbyr.)

The path passes to the left of the Pinnacles eventually entering woods by a stile or gate. Follow the well worn footpath ahead through the trees then across the bracken covered hillside below Clogwyn Mawr. Climb over a ladder stile beside a gate and follow the obvious footpath ahead.

There are superb views back down the valley from the top of the rise to the Snowdon group and Moel Siabod with Llynnau Mymbyr and Capel Curig in the valley.

Cross a small footbridge and bear left onto a well-worn footpath which eventually skirts a large flat area of peat which may once have been a lake. Beyond this, the path rises gradually to a broad col where it splits. Take the left fork which shortly gives fine views down into the Crafnant valley and across to the craggy tops of Creigiau Gleision.

As you begin to descend you are treated to a bird's eye view of Llyn Crafnant and the surrounding hills.

There are several hanging valleys on the west side of the Conwy Valley, all running in a northeasterly direction and displaying the classic glacial features which can be seen here. They were fed by ice flowing from the higher slopes of the eastern Carneddau but were severed from the Conwy Valley and left as hanging valleys by the main Conwy Valley glacier. The result is a number of

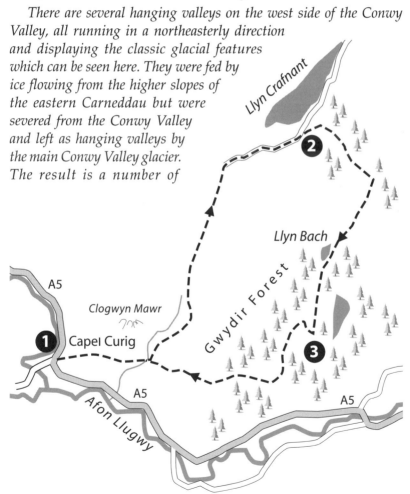

Looking back to Snowdon from the path to Llyn Crafnant

beautiful hidden valleys, often containing lakes. Crafnant is probably the most attractive of these; being slightly lower and more sheltered than its neighbours, it has more tree cover and is a blaze of colour in the autumn months.

Follow the obvious path down into the valley to a stile beside a gateway in a wall. Go left through the gateway then bear half-right through a small open field to join a lane by a gate. Turn right along the lane.

2. In about ¾ mile bear right onto the signed footpath to Llyn 'Geirionydd' near to a telephone box. After about 200 yards you meet the path from 'Cynllwyd' coming up on the left, turn right here and follow the well worn path over the shoulder of Mynydd Deulyn.

At the top of the rise, a stile leads over the wall and a short drop brings you to a forestry road. Turn right along the forest road and keep right at the first bend. After about 200 yards, where the road bends to the left, turn right at a stile and gate onto a second forest road which takes you out of the forest area (NB – the first 250 yards of this forest road is not a public right of way but it seems to be used regularly to link the two forest areas without a problem). Enter the plantations again at a large gate across the track. At the next junction bear right and pass the quiet pool of Llyn Bychan (*little lake*). Follow a good forest road now for about ½ mile.

3. Take the first forest road on the right and follow this as it contours the hillside below a series of vegetated crags. Ignore a path on the right after about a mile and as you begin to emerge from the trees the striking outline of Moel Siabod comes into view to the left.

Where the track bends right as it leaves the trees, bear left to a stile over the wall which leads onto a rough path enclosed by crumbling stone walls and a fence. This path is well used and where the walls give way, small wooden posts and stiles mark the route. Soon, a short rise leads up to a stile and you are once again in open pasture with a fine view of the mountains ahead. Keep ahead at a crossing track and follow the wooden posts which mark the right of way across a wet area to the footbridge used earlier. Retrace the outward journey back to Capel Curig to complete the walk.

Nant Ffrancon

Distance: 5¹/₂ miles

A walk up onto the lower slopes of the Carneddau with excellent views of the northern and eastern cwms of the Glyderau. The return loop is made by a quiet lane and a new cycleway—Lon Las Ogwen. Some careful route finding is required at one point on the upper section, otherwise paths are excellent throughout.

Start: One or two cars can be parked in a small layby adjacent to the entrance to 'Ogwen Bank Caravan Park and Country Club' near Bethesda on the A5.

Grid ref: 627 654 (Landranger 115, Outdoor Leisure sheet 17)

The walk

1. Take the signed footpath into woods immediately opposite the Ogwen Bank sign. Rise through the trees to cross a track and continue with conifers to the right. At the top of the rise go through a small metal gate in the wall and bear right to a forest track where a number of paths and tracks meet. Turn right and follow a good path through the woods of Braich Melyn

During the winter months the deciduous woods higher up to your right will allow views over to the massive slate quarries which sprawl over the lower slopes of Carnedd y Filiast.

After a stile the path enters open, gorse covered grazing fields. Continue until the path turns sharp left (large boulder to the left). Turn left here and follow the path which becomes fainter as you continue to rise. As the slope begins to level and before you reach the conifer woods at the top of the rise, turn right onto a narrow but clearly visible footpath which crosses at right angles.

Rise from here keeping to the right of a sheep fold, then stay beside a stone wall on the right.

There are excellent views from here across Nant Ffrancon to the peaks of (r to l) Carnedd y Filiast with its massive slabs, Mynydd Perfedd, Foel Goch and Y Garn. The higher summits of the Glyderau and its rocky ridges span the head of the valley—Bristly Ridge, Castell y Gwynt, Y Gribin and the imposing head-wall of Cwm Idwal.

The glacial origin of these northeastern cwms can be plainly seen from here. They were formed in a late glacial period and contained small active glaciers long after the large valley glacier which carved Nant Ffrancon had disappeared. Southwesterly winds caused snow to accumulate and linger where the sun was unable to melt it for much of the year. The result today is a marked contrast between the southwestern and northeastern slopes of almost all the mountains in Snowdonia. Several valleys have quite sizeable terminal moraines at their mouth. These mark the lower limit of an active glacier and are composed of the

The peaks of the Glyderau above Nant Ffrancon

debris transported by the ice before it melts. One of the finest can be seen almost opposite below Carnedd y Filiast.

Continue beside the wall eventually passing above a small conifer wood on the right. Cross two streams, then bear right to cross a third stream, where, immediately after the stream, there is an old iron gate hidden in the corner of the wall which leads into a sheepfold. A wooden ladder stile takes you out of the sheepfold and a left turn will take you to a second stile in the fence. After this stile, walk straight ahead (towards the pointed top of Foel Goch) following a footpath created and marked by the National Trust (wooden posts carrying their logo mark the route). You are directed down the hillside at first, then the path curves left taking a more contouring line until you join a much more obvious track cut into the hillside. This is known as the 'Priest's Path'.

The Priest's Path is thought to have been used by priests, from a religious settlement near Aber, to visit churches at Ty Gwyn below us in Nant Ffrancon and Nant Peris by an extension of the path which climbed between Foel Goch and Mynydd Perfedd. If this is true it must only have been used during the summer months, perhaps when families had moved up the valley with their cattle to the summer pastures, as this route would have been both difficult and hazardous in icy winter conditions.

Follow the path diagonally down the hillside until, just above a farmhouse (Ty Gwyn) down the slope to the right, a sharp right turn can be made which leads to a gate in the corner of the field. Go through the gate and drop to the road (A5).

2. Cross the road and take the signed footpath opposite. Cut through the field to the footbridge over Afon Ogwen and follow the well worn footpath beyond the bridge to the lane. Turn right and follow the lane.

This road, now known as the 'old road' was built by Richard Pennant (Lord Penrhyn), whose vast estate included all Nant Ffrancon, much of the Ogwen Valley to Capel Curig and all the land bordering Afon Ogwen down to its mouth near Penrhyn Castle. Previously there had only been a packhorse route—probably little more than a rough footpath by modern standards—up the eastern side of the valley and along the northern shore of Llyn Ogwen. Pennant built his new road in 1791 and by choosing the western side of the valley he avoided the treacherous screes below Braich Ty Du and enabled the glaciated rock step below Llyn Ogwen to be overcome without too much trouble. Travelling down the valley on the A5 today, we hardly notice this feature, but in the past it was a major obstacle.

By 1800 he had extended the road to Capel Curig and then to Ty Hyll (the Ugly House) near Betws-y-Coed. Within a few years the Capel Curig Turnpike Trust built a link to Pentrefoelas where coaches bound for Holyhead had been coming to, before heading north to Llanrwst. This new road provided a route which avoided the hazardous negotiation of the coast road between Conwy and Penmaenmawr and it was quickly adopted by the Irish Mail coaches. Within a few years this previously remote mountain valley had been transformed into a busy highway. When Thomas Telford was commissioned to improve the London to Holyhead road, he chose almost the same route except here at Nant Ffrancon where he reverted to the east side of the valley which allowed him to reduce the previously steep gradient to less than 1 in 20.

Pennant was also instrumental in bringing another great change to the valley which came in the form of the gigantic slate quarry which now sprawls across the northern slopes of Carnedd y Filiast (visible at the beginning of the walk) and the growth and development of the town of Bethesda. Small-scale quarrying had been carried out near the mouth of the valley since the sixteenth century but it was Pennant who began quarrying on a large scale in 1790. One of the big advantages was that Pennant's tenant farmers could now supplement their income with extra work in the quarry.

The quarry brought in such a vast fortune, that Richard's successor George Hay Dawkins Pennant was able to commission the building of Penrhyn Castle near Bangor which now belongs to the National Trust. The quarry expanded rapidly until over 3,000 men were employed there by 1863. The higher wages which could be earned, compared to those of an agricultural worker, were offset by poor health and a low life expectancy. The average age at death of men who worked in the splitting sheds was just 48.

The quarry remained prosperous until 1880 with a peak in 1862. Demand slumped towards the close of the nineteenth century and the slate industry nationally began a slow decline. At this time the owners tried to introduce new working methods which led to a period of strikes and lockouts bringing the business to its knees, although it has never closed and is still worked today on a small scale for decorative stone.

3. Continue down the road to the 'Lon Las Ogwen' sign. This is a cycle and walking trail linking Bangor with Bethesda and Nant Ffrancon. The path skirts the edge of the massive slate spoil heaps before running close to Afon Ogwen. At the first bridge turn right across the river and pass Ogwen Bank to return to point 1.

Llyn Padarn

Distance: 6 *miles*

A walk through the woods of the Padarn Country Park with excellent views of Snowdon and Llyn Padarn. There is also impressive quarry scenery near Llanberis. Good footpaths throughout.

Start: Begin the walk in the village of Brynrefail, just north of the outlet of Llyn Padarn. Parking is available in a loop of the old road immediately before the bridge over Afon Rhythallt. (Alternative start at the Vivian Quarry car park at the eastern end of Llyn Padarn, grid ref: 586 605.)

Grid ref: 558 623 (Landranger 115, Outdoor Leisure sheet 17).

The walk

1. Cross the bridge and where the road forks bear left into Brynrefail. In about 300 yards turn right into a lane signed 'Tai Felin'. Follow the road past a row of houses on the left and immediately before the drive to 'Tyn Twll' turn left through a kissing gate. Climb stone steps beside the wall, then pass through a small field to a lane. Turn right along the lane which becomes little more than a path beyond a farm on the left. Follow the rising path between walls until you pass through a gap in the wall to join a crossing path just beyond ruins on the right.

2. Turn right here, walk past the ruined buildings and rise gradually to enter the 'Padarn Country Park' at a small iron gate. Follow the obvious path through a mixture of heather, gorse and young birch trees until you have a magnificent, and much

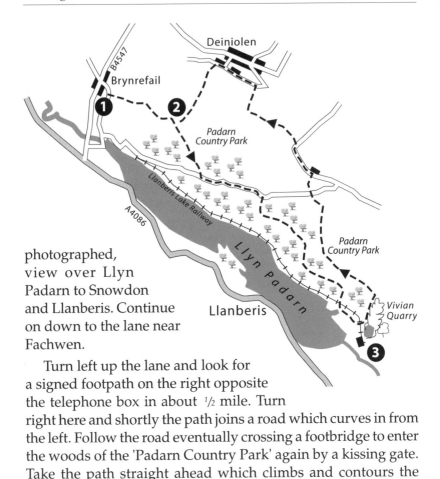

photographed,
view over Llyn
Padarn to Snowdon
and Llanberis. Continue
on down to the lane near
Fachwen.

Turn left up the lane and look for
a signed footpath on the right opposite
the telephone box in about ¹/₂ mile. Turn
right here and shortly the path joins a road which curves in from
the left. Follow the road eventually crossing a footbridge to enter
the woods of the 'Padarn Country Park' again by a kissing gate.
Take the path straight ahead which climbs and contours the
hillside passing a viewpoint overlooking the lake.

*Oak woods similar to these would have covered much of Snowdonia
away from the coast until the Middle Ages. A gradual clearing of the
tree cover which began in the valleys and then continued onto the hills
was followed by the introduction of cattle and later sheep which were
able to graze even high crags previously inaccessible to cattle. This
prevented the forests from regenerating and the present empty and often
barren landscape is the result. The absence of tree cover has led in many
areas to the development of extensive bogs whose acid soil also inhibits
the regeneration of woodland.*

As you near the country park visitor centre and slate museum buildings, bear right past the Quarry Hospital (first building) then down a large flight of steps immediately in front of the Hospital Visitor Centre. This takes you down to the lakeside picnic area.

There is a large car park here along with craft shops and W.C. facilities. This could be used as an alternative start to the walk.

The area around Llyn Padarn and Llyn Peris was being quarried for slate as early as the reign of Queen Elizabeth I, but the huge scars on the southern slopes of Elidir Fawr which we see today are the result of an increase in demand during the latter half of the eighteenth century which led to the establishing of the Dinorwig Slate Quarry in 1787. Operations then took a more organised form and by 1791 output had reach over two and a half million slates per year. This activity was so intense that it dominated the port of Caernarfon forcing Lord Penrhyn, who owned the Penrhyn Slate Quarry in the adjacent valley of Nant Ffrancon, to build his own port (Porth Penrhyn) near Bangor.

A short railway was built between Dinorwig and the port at Caernarfon to transport slates swiftly and cheaply. This remained in use throughout the nineteenth century and was finally closed in 1961. Since 1971 the Llanberis Lake Railway has carried visitors along the most attractive section of this route—the two mile section beside Llyn Padarn.

3. Walk across the car park towards the Vivian Diving Centre and turn right onto a rising path immediately before the archway leading to the Vivian Quarry. Walk up the incline then turn left onto a road.

Within a few yards you are looking down into the deep slate-blue water of the Vivian Quarry which is over 60 feet deep. The smooth quarry sides which rise for several hundred feet above the water are frequented by rock climbers.

Immediately after the quarry turn right up steps on the signed path. Climb a series of stone steps linking old levels with the Vivian Quarry close by to the right. Do not be tempted by any of

Snowdon and Llyn Padarn from above Fachwen

the stiles you will see to the right. These are used by climbers to access the steep quarry face.

At the top of the steep climb a stile leads onto a path which leads across the top of the quarry. Turn left here, cross a second stile and bear left onto a dirt road. Follow this until it bends right. Bear left onto a footpath here keeping beside the fence on the left. A little further on bear left over a stile in the fence into the 'Padarn Country Park'. Shortly, turn right over a ladder stile into the oak woods again. Take the path straight ahead—in 50 yards bear left and at a junction of paths lower down bear right.

Eventually the path follows an embankment and footbridge and leads out of the woods and the 'Padarn Country Park' by gates which take you onto a dirt road. Follow this up to the lane and turn left. At the next T junction, take the signed footpath opposite to 'Deiniolen'. At the next lane turn left and follow the road past houses on the right and round a bend. Turn into the second lane on the left which carries the dead end road sign. At the end of the lane fork left passing the sign to 'Tyddyn Du'. A kissing gate at the end of the path leads onto the open hillside with a broad view to the village of Deiniolen and out across Anglesey directly ahead. Follow the traversing path round the hill, then turn right through a kissing gate and descend the obvious footpath to the village. At the road turn left and continue until you leave the cottages behind. Look for a track on the left immediately before a cottage also on the left. There is a footpath sign here and if you reach a lane on the right you have come too far.

Turn left down this track. There is a kissing gate beside a gate in a few yards to confirm that you are on the right route. Follow the track to a farm and turn right onto a signed footpath contained between stone walls and small fields. After a kissing gate look for a stile and gap in the wall on the right (about 300 yards). This was used in the early part of the walk. Turn right and retrace the outward journey. If you started the walk at the Vivian Quarry car park walk straight ahead here and continue from point 2.

Llyn Gwynant

Distance: *5 1/2 miles*

A walk which encircles the beautiful mountain lake of Llyn Gwynant. There are some lovely picnic spots above the lake and some stunning views of Snowdon near the end of the walk. Excellent footpaths throughout.

Start: Start at the National Park car park for the Watkin Path approach to Snowdon. This lies between Llyn Dinas and Llyn Gwynant on the A498.
Grid ref: 628 508 (Landranger 115, Outdoor Leisure sheet 17).

The walk

1. Turn right out of the car park and follow the road for about half a mile. About 100 yards before a stone house on the left, turn left through a small wooden gate. Walk beside the river to a footbridge and cross over. Turn right immediately after the bridge onto a well used footpath which runs parallel to the river. Shortly, the river bears right and the path forks—keep left passing to the left of a small tree covered knoll to a gap in the wall. The path now rises to a mound of rust covered stones which form the waste from a small trial mine nearby. It is also an excellent spot to look for samples of iron pyrites or 'Fool's Gold'.

The well-worn footpath continues to rise before descending to a small ruin. Cross a stream a little further on, then rise through the trees to a point overlooking the lake. The path descends from here to a ladder stile over the wall close to the point at which Afon Glaslyn enters the lake. Cross the stile and continue with the wall to your right eventually passing through an area of huge

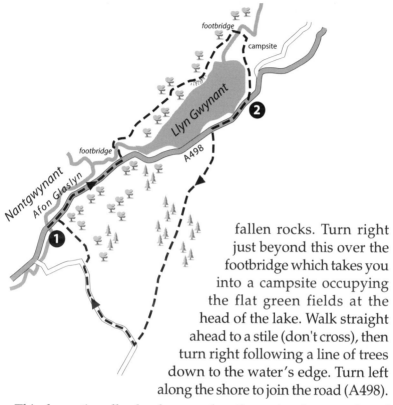

fallen rocks. Turn right just beyond this over the footbridge which takes you into a campsite occupying the flat green fields at the head of the lake. Walk straight ahead to a stile (don't cross), then turn right following a line of trees down to the water's edge. Turn left along the shore to join the road (A498).

This dramatic valley has been used as the setting for a number of Arthurian film productions in recent years. The mix of native woodland, lake and mountain make it a perfect location. When this route was initially explored filming was in progress beside the lake for the TV film Merlin *with Sam Neil as Merlin and Miranda Richardson as Queen Mab. The same location was chosen for some of the scenes from* First Knight *which starred Richard Gere and Sean Connery.*

Ironically, there is little of historic interest here today—no major events are known to have taken place here and the only early remains consist of a Roman camp at the head of the valley near Pen y Gwryd and the Dark Age fortress which existed at Dinas Emrys further down the valley towards Beddgelert.

One reason for this may well be its location, deep within the

View to the southern flanks of Snowdon near the end of the walk

mountain wilderness of Eryri in the heart of the ancient kingdom of Gwynedd. As such it would undoubtedly have been used as a safe retreat by the people of Gwynedd in times of trouble.

2. Turn right along the road and after about 500 yards look for a signed footpath on the left. This follows a stoney track beyond a gate which begins to rise before veering right after 100 yards or so. The right of way leaves the track here and continues straight ahead up stone steps with a wall to the left. Higher up you meet the track again where it curves in from the right.

There are fine views from here back towards the lake, with the slopes of Gallt y Wenalt rising toward the shoulder of Y Lliwedd and the backs of the Glyderau at the head of the valley.

Continue beside the wall to meet the track again which you should now follow. The angle eases and when the wall on the right ends, follow the track as it bends sharp right towards farm buildings. Ignore the signed footpath to the right here which will take you down to the Youth Hostel, instead, turn left along the track through a gap in the wall. Immediately after the gap, bear half-left off the track and keep beside the wall to enter conifers in the field corner. Take the well-worn footpath through the trees for almost ½ mile.

A ladder stile takes you out of trees and into an area of rhododendrons. The footpath is still obvious and eventually leads to a gate in the wall. Beyond the gate the path leads through a grazing field. Walk straight ahead eventually crossing Afon Llynedno by a wooden footbridge. Bear left after the bridge to a ladder stile, then follow a track to emerge in a quiet lane.

Turn right and walk down the lane with dramatic views of the Snowdon massif directly ahead.

After about ¾ mile, bear right onto a signed footpath into woods again. An overgrown stone bridge takes you over the river and up to a T junction with an access road. Turn left here and follow the road back to the car park.

Aberglaslyn & Llyn Dinas

Distance: *5³/₄ miles*

This is a popular well-walked route over moderate hillsides with fine views of the Snowdon range and Llyn Dinas. Return is made by riverside paths to Beddgelert and the recently improved path through the well known Pass of Aberglaslyn. Paths are excellent throughout although one section of the Aberglaslyn path requires a short moderate scramble over rocks beside the river which can not be avoided.

Start: Begin the walk in the Nantmor Picnic area where there is pay and display parking available, along with WC facilities.

Grid ref: 597 462 (Landranger 115, Outdoor Leisure sheet 17).

The walk

1. Walk out of the car park past the WC block and through the arch under the trackbed of the Welsh Highland Railway. Continue ahead to pick up a path which makes its way up the little valley of Cwm Bychan. At first you pass through woods with the stream to your right before more open ground beyond a gate in the wall.

The path continues up the valley passing numerous remains from mining in the area, from small trial excavations to the rusting supports of an old cableway. Higher up, don't be tempted by the valley to the left, instead, carry on straight ahead eventually reaching the skyline where a ladder stile leads over the fence.

In clear conditions the view from here is dominated by the southern

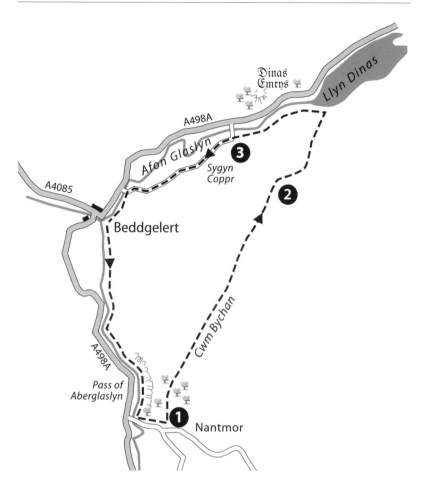

flanks of Snowdon and its satellite peaks of Yr Aran and Y Lliwedd, while the rocky crest of Crib Goch can be see through the gap known as Bwlch y Saethiau, meaning 'pass of the arrows'. This name links it with the last battle of King Arthur and is one of the supposed sites of his of his final conflict with Mordred.

2. Turn left here and follow the path to a junction where there is a fingerpost. Turn right signed to 'Llyn Dinas' and follow the well constructed footpath down hill. Just above the lake the path steepens and zig-zags down to the water's edge.

Snowdon from the path above Llyn Dinas

Llyn Dinas means 'lake of the city' or 'fortress' and is almost certainly a reference to nearby Dinas Emrys, one of the most important Dark Age sites in this part of Wales. It is known to have been the site of a timber castle in the early post-Roman period and there are remains of even earlier, possibly Iron Age, defences. The scant remains to be found on the hilltop today are thought to be those of a thirteenth century stone tower.

Turn left by the outflow of the lake through a kissing gate and, ignoring the footbridge on the right, follow a good path ahead beside the river with the flat topped crag of Dinas Emrys ahead.

Although little is known about the occupants of Dinas Emrys for sure, it would almost certainly have been used by the many Welsh Princes prior to the Edwardian Conquest although the need for a stronghold this far into the mountains can not have been great once the threat from Irish raids had been removed.

Dinas Emrys is the location of the mythical confrontation between Vortigern, the high king of Britain and Ambrosius (Emrys in Welsh) the British leader responsible for Vortigern's exile and leader of the British resistance to the Saxon colonisation of eastern Britain. For a full account of this meeting see pages 14 and 15.

Pass a stone-built house on the left and eventually join the access road to 'Sygyn Coppr'. Turn left along the road, then turn right along a track just before the souvenir shop as indicated by the footpath sign.

3. Follow the track to a gate and join a narrow tarmac lane. Walk along this lane until it bends right over the river to join the A498.

Here, stone steps lead left over the wall immediately before the bridge and onto a riverside footpath. Stay beside the river, crossing an access road, until you come to the metal footbridge in Beddgelert where Afon Glaslyn and Afon Colwyn meet. Do not cross the river, instead, turn left and keep beside the river until you cross the trackbed of the Welsh Highland Railway (almost ¹/₂ mile). The trackbed used to provide a footpath link

Llyn Dinas

back to the car park at Nantmor, but the tunnel has now been closed as the track is rebuilt. Follow the path which has recently been improved beside the river. As this enters the gorge of Aberglaslyn a short scramble around a rock corner adds interest but might be intimidating to some. Thereafter wooden walkways take you over the rocky sections. This is a lovely section of the walk.

The Pass of Aberglaslyn is a well known beauty spot, made popular by Victorian travellers, writers and painters. It is almost impossible to find a book about North Wales, particularly from the early half of the twentieth century, which does not contain a photograph from the bridge at the mouth of the gorge.

As you emerge from the gorge at Aberglaslyn, do not go through the kissing gate onto the road, instead, turn left and follow the path back to the car park at Nantmor.

Beddgelert Forest

Distance: *7¼ miles*

An exploration of forest tracks and mountain passes at the head of the remote Cwm Pennant. Some sections require detailed route finding and can be boggy during wet weather. Otherwise footpaths and forest tracks are well used and easily followed.

Start: Begin the walk either at the car park provided for the Rhyd Ddu Snowdon Path, just to the south of the village of Rhyd Ddu on the A4085 (Grid ref: 571 526), or from a layby on the B4418 near 'Tan y Llyn' immediately west of Rhyd Ddu and start from point 2.
(Grid ref: 571 525). (Landranger 115, Outdoor Leisure sheet 17).

The walk

1. Opposite the car park entrance a kissing gate leads onto a footpath paved with flat stones which crosses a damp flat field with the dramatic profile of Y Garn, the northeastern terminus of the Nantlle Ridge, directly ahead. At a stream bear left to a footbridge with a stone cottage on the right. Cross the driveway and shortly join it again a little further on continuing to the road (B4418).

2. Turn left here onto a signed bridleway. Follow the obvious path ignoring paths to the right and left, eventually reaching a stile and gate after a short climb. A little further on, bear left onto a faint path where there are a number of white arrows painted onto rocks (the Nantlle Ridge path climbs steeply to Y Garn, the first summit, from here). After 50 yards or so, there are more arrows on nearby rocks to confirm that you are on the right route. This path climbs steadily in the direction of a low point on the skyline to the left of the Nantlle Ridge. Cross a stream and a little further on enter conifer plantations by a stile or gate.

At the first forest road continue straight ahead to join a second road near a small bridge. Turn left over the bridge, then immediately right onto a broad forest road. At the first T junction turn right and in about 50 yards turn left onto an ascending rocky path.

The tiny settlement of Dolbenmaen lies at the mouth of Cwm Pennant and was, in the past, a settlement of some importance being the site of a castle held by the independent Princes of Gwynedd. Gruffydd ap Cynan, Owain Gwynedd and Llywelyn Fawr are prominent names which come down to us from that period. The castle was built in the style of the Norman motte and bailey and was almost certainly constructed of timber, as there are now no remains other than the mound on which the castle stood. In the early

The southwest flanks of Snowdon from the Beddgelert Forest

thirteenth century it was replaced by a much more substantial fortress at Criccieth, the remains of which can still be seen. Another one of Llywelyn's castles can be seen at Llyn Peris near Llanberis. Communication between these fortresses would always have been by the shortest route. This path may well be part of an ancient route between the two castles, or in more recent times, from the mines at Rhyd Ddu or Betws Garmon.

At the top of the rise emerge from the trees and look to the left for a fine view of the southwestern flanks of the Snowdon group. From the valley at the start of the walk, Snowdon looked quite low and unimpressive but as you climb it seems to grow until it looks all of its 3,560 feet. To the right is the graceful cone of Yr Aran with the triple top of Y Lliwedd visible over Snowdon's south ridge.

Continue to a gate from where there is a fine view down Cwm Pennant to Cardigan Bay. The path forks here. Keep left down through old mine workings. Stay in the bottom of the valley and don't be tempted to follow any of the paths on the right which only lead along the many mine levels. Lower down, bear left onto a well worn path past a deep shaft on the left. This path traverses to the pass below Moel Lefn (Bwlch Cwm-trwsgl).

To the right there is a fine profile of the Nantlle Ridge—in particular the rocky northeast ridge of Craig Cwm Silyn.

Skirt a marshy area by keeping close to a wall to reach the highest point of the pass. Bear left through a gap in the wall and enter the Beddgelert Forest again. Descend a rocky and often wet path to a forest road. Turn left here and after 100 yards or so, look for a narrow but well used footpath on the right. Follow this path through the trees keeping right at two forks to leave the woods by a gap in the wall. Follow the obvious traversing path (marked by well spaced blue posts) straight ahead with fine views of the Snowdon group to the left.

A stile in the fence ahead takes you back into the woods again. At the first forest road turn left, then after a few yards turn right onto a narrow footpath which takes you directly down the hillside crossing a number of forest roads again. Keep descending until you cross over a wall into a small rough field with a house ('Hafod Ruffydd Uchaf') on the right. Walk along the right-hand field edge passing the cottage to a stile which leads onto a forest road. Turn left along the road keeping right at a fork in 100 yards or so. Pass a second stone house on the right and continue along the forest road with good views ahead to Snowdon in clear conditions. At the next junction bear right and follow this road down to a bridge over Afon Cwm-Du. From here the track bends right and shortly reaches a T junction with a lane. Turn left here past a house ('Hafod Ruffydd Isaf') and follow a straight forest road for about ½ mile ignoring forest roads to the left.

3. Where the forest road joins the main road on the right ('Pont Cae'r Gors'), turn left onto a second forest road which rises gently. Take the second road on the right at the top of the rise (just over ¼ mile). Where this forks in about 350 yards keep right again.

Moel Hebog from Beddgelert Forest

Where the road turns sharply to the left, go ahead on the bend onto a narrow footpath. Shortly a small stile leads over the fence. Go ahead over the stile and in a few yards cross a wall into woods again. Turn left now and keep beside the wall.

At old mine workings bear left and cross a ladder stile behind a ruined building. Bear to the right for a few yards then contour the hillside passing a small flooded quarry on the right. There is no visible path from here so pick you way through the spoil heaps aiming to the left of a distant farm. Pass through a gap in the far wall, cross a stream and keep to the left of fenced fields on the right. Head for a gate in the top right-hand corner of the field. Go through this and keep right along the field edge to join the outward route. Turn right and retrace your steps back to Rhyd Ddu.

Betws Garmon

Distance: *7½ miles*

A walk in a less frequented part of Snowdonia. Moorland walking with wide views is followed by forest paths. A return is made through the farmland of Betws Garmon and Waunfawr. Footpaths are generally good.

Start: Take the lane signed to 'Rhosgadfan' about 500 yards south of the 'Snowdonia Parc' public house on the A4085 between Waunfawr and Betws Garmon. Follow the rising lane for about 1 mile until it levels off on the open hillside. Parking is available on the right.
Grid ref: 514 583 (Landranger 115, Outdoor Leisure sheet 17).

The walk

1. Walk back along the lane (to the left if you parked on the north side of the road) and after a few yards bear right onto a track which heads towards a white cottage. Shortly, bear right again and follow a track which runs beside the wall on the left. Where the track bends left to 'Penrallt' continue on the path beside the wall and at a fork a little further on keep right across the open heather covered moors. Pass a group of wall enclosed fields on the right, then continue on the path directly ahead which rises to the rounded summit of Moel Smytho.

This little hilltop is a fine viewpoint. To the southeast you will see the rounded ridge of the Moel Eilio and the impressive northern cwm of Mynydd Mawr, with the summit of Snowdon between. Further west, part of the Nantlle Ridge can be seen along with the rounded hills of Gryn Ddu and Bwlch Mawr on the Lleyn Peninsula. The more shapely

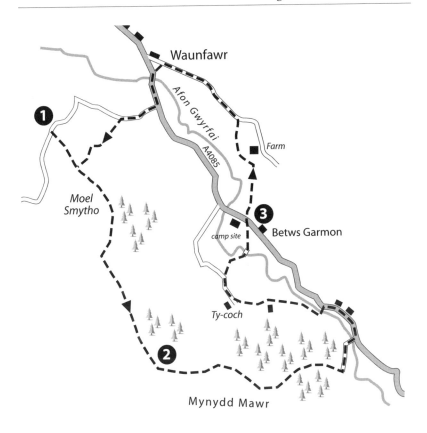

tops of Yr Eifl can also be seen, while to the north much of Anglesey is visible.

Continue over the summit and drop towards conifer woods. Ignore a ladder stile leading over the fence into the trees on the left here, instead, bear right on a broad path which heads southwst in the direction of a farm on the far hillside below slag heaps. At a T junction with an obvious track where there is a red topped post, turn left. Shortly the path forks; keep right here following a path across the heather moors marked occasionally by red topped posts. Make a short detour round an old trial level (a long shallow ditch reaching down the hillside) and continue on the path still marked by the red topped posts. Level with the end of slag heaps on the right and near a large rock also on the right, turn left down towards a wall.

2. Turn right to walk beside the wall. Where this turns left at a broad marshy col below the steep final slopes of Mynydd Mawr, keep left with the wall. This contours the hillside above Betws Garmon until you are directly below the dark glacial hollow of Cwm Du with its imposing headwall up to the right. Look for a ladder stile on the left here, cross it and follow the path beside woods on the left until a second stile leads into the trees. After a short rise a good path drops steeply through the trees to emerge at a gate with a view up the valley to Llyn Cwellyn, with the commanding crags of Castell Cidwm falling almost sheer to the lake. The pyramidal peak beyond the lake is Yr Aran, one of the satellite peaks of Snowdon.

Walk directly down through bracken to a track. Turn left and follow the track over the railway and the river to the road. Turn left and walk along the road to Betws Garmon. Turn left here onto a signed footpath which takes you over the river again by a wooden footbridge. Bear right immediately after the footbridge and walk beside the river. Pass through a gap in the far wall and bear half-left to a ladder and cross the railway (Welsh Highland Railway).

This railway was originally part of the North Wales Narrow Gauge Railways which ran between Dinas Junction near Caernarfon and Rhyd Ddu at the southern end of Llyn Cwellyn. The line came up from Llanwnda to Waunfawr and passed through Betws Garmon, then along the shore of Llyn Cwellyn to Rhyd Ddu. In the 1920s a link was built between its terminus at Rhyd Ddu and the Croesor Tramway which ran from Croesor to Porthmadog. The old car park for the Rhyd Ddu Snowdon Path occupied part of the track which then followed the line of the modern road before making the long descent to Beddgelert. Passing to the west of the village it ran beside Afon Glaslyn to the tunnel between Aberglaslyn and Nantmor. From there it crossed the recently reclaimed marshes of Traeth Mawr to join the Croesor Tramway. The Croesor Tramway was restored a number of years ago and at the time of writing

Looking towards Snowdon from the slopes below Mynydd Mawr

work is underway to restore the entire line right through from Caernarfon to Porthmadog.

Continue ahead by the wall on the left to another ladder stile and gate, then make a slight rise before curving left as indicated by an arrow on a low post. After a gate, turn right towards a farm turning right over a stile immediately before the house. Bear left through a field to a stile which leads onto the farm access road. Cross the track and stream to a second stile which leads into fields again. Walk diagonally through the centre of the field and along the right-hand edge in the following field. Walk through a small field to a kissing gate in front of a farmhouse and turn right down the access road.

Keep right at the next junction and at 'Hafod y Wern' turn right through a kissing gate into fields again. Walk through the centre of a large field following a faint track which bears right by the river and heads towards a ruin. At the ruin turn left over a footbridge and walk straight through a campsite (the exact line of the right of way follows what was once a hedgeline although it may be impractical to walk this line). Follow yellow waymarkers eventually crossing the Welsh Highland Railway by the site access road. Bear left with the site road then turn right between buildings to a kissing gate which leads onto the road opposite 'Betws Inn' B&B. Turn left along the road past the site entrance ('Bryn Gloch').

3. Cross the road and take the signed footpath opposite to the left of the church. A kissing gate at the end of a short path enclosed by iron railings leads into fields again. Walk straight ahead, then keep to the left-hand fence in the second larger field to a kissing gate and footbridge. Take a direct line from here towards farm buildings. After passing through a kissing gate in the wall, bear half-right up to a ruined farm building. Go through a gateway immediately in front of the ruin and bear left to walk beside the wall on your left. At a kissing gate in the far corner keep straight ahead with a rocky, tree-covered crag to your right. Keep ahead through fields with two more kissing gates and a stone stile. Immediately after the stile, bear half-left to a gap in the hedge where there is a small stone footbridge and walk through the following field to a kissing gate into a lane. Turn left and walk along the quiet lane for about ³/₄ mile to the village of Waunfawr.

Where there is housing on both sides of the road, turn left onto a signed footpath between gardens which leads back to the A4085. Turn left at the road and just after the 'Snowdonia Parc' public house, turn right into the lane signed 'Rhosgafan 2'. The lane can be followed back to the car park or a path on the left (signed to 'Y Fron 3¹/₄ m') can be taken as a more strenuous alternative. The path, which is marked by red topped posts, rises through bracken at first, then more steeply through broken woodland to emerge high on the hillside overlooking Waunfawr. Cross a stile on the left and bear right to pass the ruins of an old hill farm and make your way to a gate in the wall which leads onto the open heather covered moors again. Turn right to return to the car park.

Penrhyndeudraeth

Distance: *6 miles*

Old lanes, field paths and forest tracks are used to explore this quiet corner in the beautiful Vale of Ffestiniog.

Start: Park in one of the three laybys created from loops of the old road midway between Maentwrog and Penrhyndeudraeth on the A487.

Grid ref: 635 402. (Landranger 115, Outdoor Leisure sheet 18).

The walk

1. Turn right along the road and look for a signed footpath on the left just before a stone house on the right. Drop down the bank to a ladder stile and walk beside the stream for a few yards (ignore a stile in the fence on the right) before turning right to follow a grass path to a lane. Turn right along the lane.

This lane was once the main route between Penrhyndeudraeth and Maentwrog and is shown on Evans' map published in the 1790s. The route followed an old seawall which can still be seen enclosing fields to the east of here bordering Afon Dwyryd. It then passed along this now quite little valley to enter the village of Penrhyndeudraeth near the station. With the building of the Cob at Porthmadog a new road was built taking a more direct line and this lovely old lane was abandoned. After a few hundred yards or so, once the noise from the main road has faded, you will begin to get some idea of just how quiet and isolated this peninsula was in the days before the grand schemes of Alexanda Madocks and Samuel Holland placed it on a main highway.

About 85 yards after 'Bryn Dwyryd', a farmhouse on the right, turn right through a gate onto a signed footpath. Follow a track along the field edge and pass to the right of ruined outbuildings to where (about 30 yards) a ladder stile in the field corner leads over the fence. After the stile keep ahead along a tree covered bank for 100 yards or so, then bear half-left up the bank. Keep straight ahead now and walk directly up a bracken covered field with bits of old wall on your left and a ruined cottage on the right to stone steps leading into a small conifer wood. Follow the obvious path leftwards through the trees and down to the main road (A487).

2. Cross the road and walk down the drive to 'Blaen Cefn' caravan and camping site. Immediately before the camping field, turn left onto an enclosed path which leads around the site and eventually joins a lane. Turn left along the lane and after about 250 yards, turn right up the drive to 'Maesgwm' where there is a footpath sign. As you approach the house bear left onto a path which passes in front of the house and then behind cottages. At a junction turn right up the hill and pass under the Ffestiniog Railway to emerge in the road beside the 'Penrhyndeudraeth' sign.

The majority of Welsh place names are either dedications to early Celtic Saints or descriptive of the location. Penrhyndeudraeth comes into the latter category. It means 'headland' or 'peninsula (penrhyn) between two (deu) beaches (draeth)', a description which would have been immediately obvious before Traeth Mawr, the large tidal estuary of Afon Glaslyn to the north, was reclaimed by the grand schemes of Alexander Madocks in the early years of the nineteenth century. Prior to Madocks' activity, the estuary was tidal right up to Aberglaslyn near Beddgelert and to the nearby church of Llanfrothen.

Turn right, then right again after 10 yards into a narrow lane. Follow this lane initially uphill for almost ¾ mile as it contours the hillside high above the A487 with good views south to the northern outliers of the Rhinog hills. The lane ends at a farm yard and a number of signed paths and bridleways begin from

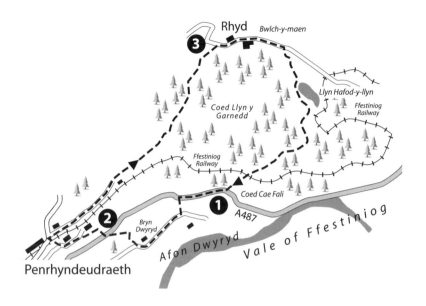

here. Ignore the bridleway to the right, instead, immediately before the farm, go through two gates straight ahead to join a grass track with iron sheds to the right. In about 30 yards pass through a gate (ignore a signed footpath rising steeply on the left). You are now on the open bracken-covered hillside and the obvious gravel path continues ahead rising slightly (ignore a signed footpath on the right). Higher up a ladder stile by a gate takes you into the woods of Coed Llyn y Garnedd. Keep left at a fork in the path after 100 yards or so and continue on the obvious path through the trees.

Pass the ruins of Pen-yr-allt (probably a 'hafod' from the eighteenth or nineteenth century) and continue on the obvious path ignoring a signed path on the left in about 25 yards and on the right about 100 yards beyond the ruins. After about 400 yards a kissing gate leads into fields. Keep ahead along field edges at first, with views straight ahead to Cnicht and the Moelwynion, then, after a small dried out pool, trend left along a bracken-covered bank to an old iron gate with fields to the right. Bear right along the fence to the lane on the edge of the village of Rhyd.

3. Turn right and walk along the lane through the village which consists of little more than a handful of attractive stone cottages. Once beyond the village, there is a short climb to Bwlch-y-maen ('pass of the stone'—possibly a reference to the large crag on the right of the road), then the road levels and there is a wet marshy area on the right backed by conifers. Immediately after this and just before the road starts to drop, there is a signed footpath on the right. Turn right onto this path and follow it around a marshy area then turn left at a junction and follow a wall up, then down to Llyn Hafod-y-llyn (the path can sometimes be a little overgrown in the late summer).

Turn right along a good forest road which rises steadily above the water with views of Moelywn Bach rising above the trees on the far side of the lake. At the top of the rise take a track which bears right for about 40 yards before turning left onto a narrow footpath through the trees. Shortly, pass through a gap in a stone wall and almost touch the track again before rising up the bank on the right. At a junction turn sharp right (do not descend to a stone building on the left) onto a rising path which levels and contours the hillside. At a junction of paths go straight ahead through an area of dense conifers for about 30 yards, then bear right and descend through more mixed open woods.

These woods contain remnants of the sessile oak woods which covered much of Snowdonia until the Middle Ages. Clearances, overgrazing and the introduction of non-indigenous species such as conifers and beech have depleted much of this native woodland, but attempts are now being made to re-establish the oak woods by means of controlled grazing and woodland management.

At a forest road turn right for about 75 yards before turning left onto a signed footpath again. Pass beside a small lake and continue the descent until an arrow directs you half-left off the path and down to a gap in a wall. A little further on a stile takes you over the Ffestiniog Railway whose narrow gauge locomotives will have been heard for some time.

The Ffestiniog Railway carries visitors for ten miles through the beautiful Vale of Ffestiniog and links the slate town of Blaenau Ffestiniog with the once flourishing seaport of Porthmadog. It was built in the 1830s in response to increased demand for slate which had been worked on a small scale in the hills around Ffestiniog for over a century. Slates were previously carried by horses to boats waiting in the upper reaches of Afon Dwyryd and then taken down stream to ships waiting near the mouth of the river at Ynys Cyngar. The railway was made possible by the recently completed Cob embankment between Penrhyndeudraeth and the quayside of William Madocks' new port at Porthmadog. From here slates were exported to the rest of Britain and Europe.

Approaching the village of Rhyd with Cnicht in the background

The decline of the slate industry in the early twentieth century led to increased dependance on passengers and summer visitors. The railway closed in 1946 and was abandoned for almost a decade before attempts to reopen it as a tourist attraction were started. Today it is the most famous and most popular narrow gauge railway in Wales.

Cross the railway and enter the National Trust woodland at Coed Cae Fali. Follow the obvious path down the hillside keeping left at the first fork and at aT junction of paths turn left through a gap in a wall and drop to a well surfaced footpath. Turn right and follow this path down to the road turning right to complete the walk.

Mara Books www.marabooks.co.uk

Mara Books publish a range of walking books for Cheshire and North Wales and have the following list to date.

North Wales
Circular Walks in the Conwy Valley
ISBN 0 9522409 7 1. A collection of 18 circular walks which explore the varied scenery of this beautiful valley from the Great Orme to Betws-y-Coed.

A pocket guide to Snowdon
ISBN 1 902512 04 9. A guide to all Snowdon's recognised routes of ascent, from the six 'Classic Paths' to the many lesser known and less frequented routes.

Coastal Walks around Anglesey Volume 1
ISBN 0 9522409 6 3. A collection of 15 walks which explore the varied scenery of Anglesey's beautiful coastline.

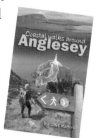

Coastal Walks around Anglesey Volume 2
ISBN 0 9522409 5 5. A companion volume to the above book, outlining 15 new walks spread around Anglesey's fascinating and beautiful coastline.

Walking the Isle of Anglesey Coastal Path
ISBN 1 902512 13 8. The official guide for the Isle of Anglesey Coastal Path. Full colour in English and Welsh.

Walking on the Lleyn Peninsula

ISBN 1 902512 00 6. A collection of 16 circular walks which explore the wild and beautiful coastline and hills of the Lleyn Peninsula.

The Mountain Men

ISBN 1 902512 11 1. This book tells the story of the pioneer rock climbers in Snowdonia in the closing decades of the nineteenth century until the outbreak of World War II.

Walking in the Clwydian Hills

ISBN 1 902512 09 X. A collection of 18 circular walks exploring the Clwydian Range Area of Outstanding Natural Beauty (AONB).

Walking in the Vale of Clwyd and Denbigh Moors

ISBN 1 902512 08 1. A collection of 18 circular walks exploring the undiscovered country between the Clwydian Hills and the Conwy Valley.

Circular walks along the Offa's Dyke Path
—Volume 1 Prestatyn to Welshpool
ISBN 1 902512 01 4.

—Volume 2 Welshpool to Hay-on-Wye
ISBN 1 902512 07 3.

The first two volumes in a series of three which sample some of the finest sections of this well known national trail.

Cheshire

Circular Walks along the Sandstone Trail

ISBN 1 902512 10 8. The Sandstone Trail is Cheshire's best known and most popular walking route. This book gives a complete route description along with 12 circular walks covering the entire trail.

A Walker's Guide to the Wirral Shore Way

ISBN 1 902512 05 7. A linear walk of 23 miles following the old coastline between Chester and Hoylake.

Circular Walks along the Gritstone Trail and Mow Cop Trail

ISBN 0 9522409 4 7. A route which follows Cheshire's eastern border along the edge of the Peak District. Following the same format as the Sandstone Trail book—a full description for both trails is combined with 12 circular walks.

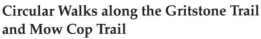

Circular Walks in Wirral

ISBN 1 902512 02 2. A collection of 15 circular walks in the coast and countryside of Wirral.